Retirement Straight Talk

Stories and Wisdom from Educators

Donald R. Draayer

ScarecrowEducation
Lanham, Maryland, and Oxford
2003

Published in the United States of America
by ScarecrowEducation, Inc.
An Imprint of The Rowman & Littlefield Publishing Group
4501 Forbes Boulevard, Suite 200, Lanham, Maryland 20706
www.scarecroweducation.com

PO Box 317
Oxford
OX2 9RU, UK

British Library Cataloguing in Publication Information Available

Library of Congress Cataloging-in-Publication Data

Draayer, Donald R. (Donald Roger), 1935–
  Retirement straight talk : stories and wisdom from educators / Donald R.
Draayer.
    p. cm.
Includes bibliographical references (p.).
  ISBN 0-8108-4727-2 (pbk. : alk. paper)
  1. Teachers—Retirement—United States. I. Title.
  LB2842.22.D73 2003
  371.1—dc21

                                                    2002155936

∞™ The paper used in this publication meets the minimum requirements of
American National Standard for Information Sciences—Permanence of Paper
for Printed Library Materials, ANSI/NISO Z39.48-1992.
Manufactured in the United States of America.

Dedicated to Mary Anne, my wife,
and other caring educators throughout the USA
who love teaching, learning, and human development
and who, in retirement, seek new venues of
expression for core values.

Contents

Preface

Poet Robert Browning captures my hope for retirement in the first verse of "Rabbi Ben Ezra:"[*]

> Grow old along with me!
> The best is yet to be,
> The last of life, for which the first was made:
> Our times are in His hand
> Who saith, "A whole I planned,
> Youth shows but half; trust God; see all,
> Nor be afraid."

AUTHOR'S PERSPECTIVE

I begin with the above verse because it weaves hope, trust, and security into the fabric of life's second half and illustrates a bold optimism in the face of new and possible fearful frontiers. For my own retirement, I appreciate powerful reminders: (1) Fresh starts are often a mixture of fantasy and vision as well as anxiety and challenge; (2) The past is like a springboard to what lies ahead; and (3) I am not alone on this journey.

Learning, for educators, is like new growth that springs forth from moist, fertile ground. It is part of creation's story, one generation to the next coming into its own. Most educators enter their profession to be the planter, the gardener, and the harvester. They have experienced in their own lives the wonderment and joy that comes from learning new skills, gaining knowledge and insight, and being a part of the transforming magic. This zest for learning continues for professionals throughout their careers and, for most, into retirement.

However, retirement is like virgin soil. The ground must be cleared, plowed, and fertilized. New possibilities must be turned over in the mind and heart. Expert opinion is needed to help answer questions about soil conditions and what will make it most productive. Learning doesn't end in retirement—it shifts to a brand new terrain.

---

[*] John Greenleaf Whittier, ed., *Song of Three Generations* (Boston: Houghton, Mifflin, 1882).

RETIREMENT MILESTONES AND QUESTIONS

An elementary child was asked at the start of school to describe her teacher and she replied: "She's of the older ages." That's me. That's you if retirement is budding or already in full bloom. What new choices are open to us? What challenges must we realistically face? What determination and commitment will get us through the retirement years with grace, joy, and hope?

For forty-five years as a teacher, principal, superintendent, university lecturer, and national educational consultant, I have seen educators come into the profession with eagerness, serve faithfully for a full career, and then move into retirement with joy and thanksgiving, as well as foreboding and disquiet. This observation prompts questions like these: Why is the act of retirement easy for some people and difficult for others? Why do many retirees move into their retirement years with confidence and sure steps, while others are plagued with a troubled spirit?

STRAIGHT TALK ABOUT RETIREMENT

This book includes straight talk by hundreds of educators, teachers, specialists, administrators, and professors about their retirement experiences. Their thoughts, feelings, and collective wisdom bring clarity to the choices, challenges, and commitments in retirement. My intent is to provide readers with a helpful road map that draws from these educators' vast experiences. Stories from their lives are like headlights that point out road signs to possible destinations and illuminate dangers and critical crossroads along the way. These stories, as well as my own, reveal the diversity of pathways into and through retirement years. My objective is not to prescribe a specific path but to illustrate possibilities in the first twenty chapters of the book.

Collective reflections and group generalizations from this study of retirees are included in chapter 21. Chapter 22 describes stages in retirement of educators. These two chapters move the reader away from the individual stories, particular insights, and phases of retirement to a big-picture format, like a large wall mural where all the interconnections are more clearly displayed. The object is to help the reader gain better perspective and to improve introspection. To illustrate such introspection, I included my own retirement story in chapter 23 with this intentional title, "Talking Turkey to Myself about Retirement." Chapter 24 summarizes retirement wisdom from educators and applauds your own retirement walk.

I believe that retirement can be a time of fulfillment. A person can learn, laugh, cry, and give to others as long as both the mind and heart function. A poignant point within the verse by poet Browning, which was cited earlier, bears repeating: "A whole I planned, Youth shows but half." Living the whole of life to its fullest and best is the end to which this book is dedicated.

ACKNOWLEDGMENTS

I am filled with awe and gratitude for the individual stories and collective wisdom of educators. With fullness of mind, body, and spirit, these educators served American youth. They continue to care and contribute by sharing their life experiences and retirement transitions. Their straight talk is now being applied in my own retirement walk.

Some stories included herein are almost verbatim. Others are compilations of story strands from many people. All are anonymous to protect privacy, except the final story in each chapter, which is my own and is titled "My Journey." This snapshot from my own retirement has two purposes: to show the strong continuity of a person's retirement story line over time and to encourage the reader to journal his or her own retirement experience as a legacy to others. Each chapter ends in parallel form with two features: (1) common-sense conclusions (the foremost definition of wisdom) and bullet points that constitute straight talk and (2) relevant questions. The latter are introspective and useful for self-reflection, private conversation, or group discussion.

I wish to credit Dr. Bob Brown, professor of educational leadership, School of Education, University of St. Thomas, and Dr. Michael Lovett, a long-time colleague and friend, who encouraged me to write and provided helpful suggestions along the way. Mary Anne, my wife, has been my constant cheerleader and companion in this effort; her patience with the travel, correspondence, and concentrated composition time has paralleled her positive and supportive attitude during all of our forty-five years together as friends and fellow educators. Dawn Thibodeau, Beth Clark, Dorothy Kleinbeck, and Karen Draayer raised questions, provided critical review, and forced clarity of thought, but always with a loving spirit. I am grateful to God for a sound mind and body, purposes to serve, and the resolve to be a good steward in every aspect of life and living.

FACING A NEW MAGNITUDE OF CHOICES

When retirement becomes a possibility, a host of choices faces educators. The good news is that nearly all 300 educators who participated in this straight talk about retirement express happiness with their choices by the end of their first year of retirement. They share that most of their dreams for retirement have become reality. However, a vast majority of these retirees also report that they underestimated the number of transitions involved in retirement. Some adjustments are subtle, even subliminal and surprising. Other adjustments are like a sledgehammer hitting hard rock—ear splitting and form changing. Section I focuses on transitions leading up to retirement.

Retirement is introduced in chapter 1 as an idea that begins with the coming together of age and societal expectation and moves from an invisible new life form to a growing presence that cannot be denied. Initially, the prospect of retirement engages the cognitive thought processes. Words relating to retirement take on new significance. Chapter 2 unveils vocabulary often used in this new awakening. Concurrently, strong emotions are triggered. Chapter 3 identifies the feelings that surge to the level of consciousness.

Behaviors begin to change and most are very natural and expected. A few behaviors may seem strange and feel uncomfortable. Chapter 4 discusses less typical manifestations. Then serious issues surface during preretirement in the form of fundamental questions. Chapter 5 identifies these questions and suggests that they must be explored fully to achieve peace of mind. Chapter 6 highlights both personal and legal steps involved regarding the formal act of retirement because, even though it seems simple on the surface, many choices exist in every aspect of follow-through.

Most educators who are nearing the end of their careers, spend more time "in retirement thinking"—that is, conversation, investigation, decision making, and follow-through. Meanwhile, the rest of life goes on until that actual day of retirement when the freedom to make choices expands exponentially. These will be covered in section II where postretirement possibilities are scrutinized.

CHAPTER ONE

Hearing the Idea of Retirement

The concept of retirement begins to take shape early in adult working life but the word remains an abstraction until many years have passed. Then something, often a little thing, turns a fuzzy, future idea into a more immediate prospect. The idea of retirement enters the mind, will not depart, and eventually turns into a life-changing decision. Stories below illustrate this point.

Diana   I received an AARP application in the mail. I threw it in the wastebasket without even reading it. However, the thought that I was eligible for membership started me thinking.

Peter   A colleague retired. Like I had done dozens of times before, I congratulated him, went to the retirement reception, and said good-bye the last day of work. It was something he said that got me thinking: "When are you going to join me?"

Alice   I had not been feeling the same for quite some time. My doctor's diagnosis was that I was entering menopause, a period of change in my life. I walked out of his office reflecting about other changes coming down the road. Included in that list was my retirement.

Many educators recall the very first time the word retirement left their lips and to whom the words were spoken. The exact moment is like a watershed in their lives that leaves an indelible mark.

Judy   My husband asked me to join him in a meeting with a financial planner. I expected to play the role of listener, but I quickly found the situation called for active participation. I hesitated to speak and clearly hedged, but I remember well hearing my tongue speak for the first time about retirement in the relative safety of husband and trusted advisor.

Samuel   My older brother and I have remained close, even though he lives all the way across the country. His job in private industry, like mine as a principal, included much conflict. He called to wish me a happy birthday, my sixtieth. I sounded off about the tension I was feeling. He asked me bluntly how many more years before my retirement.

Most educators share that from its onset the idea of retirement brings a sense of anticipation, a vision of bliss, or a longed-for freedom from work requirements and calendar restraints. It is like a wonderful promise yet to be fulfilled.

Jeff   I taught history and loved to travel. The idea of retirement conjured images in my mind of faraway places where I hoped to tour one day.

Martha   My retirement couldn't come too soon. I'd been thinking about it nearly every day for ten years. Teaching was my livelihood, not my total love. Every time I thought about retirement, I felt a surge of hope and happiness as my mind raced to all the things I could do with the free time. I was one of those people who could tell you how many school days remained until the school year ended. The last year of work was one long countdown.

Other educators report that the idea of retirement frightens or produces tension. It is like a stranger entering a room, an uncomfortable or threatening point in a conversation, or an untimely imposition in an otherwise stable, fairly predictable life.

Nora   My initial reaction to the idea was total rejection. Not me! Too soon! What's the hurry? I felt coldness in hearing the word retirement. My brain simply set the idea aside for another day, and my heart closed its door to the idea for a long time.

John   When my associates began to talk about early retirement, I turned a deaf ear. I had alimony to pay my first wife, many years of college tuition ahead of me for children from the second marriage, and a house mortgage that extended beyond my sixty-fifth birthday.

Still others relate that the idea of retirement produces both sensations of relief and foreboding—a mixed type of reaction. When work creates overload and exhaustion, retirement possibilities look like lifesavers. Conversely, when work provides great professional satisfaction and personal pleasure, retirement is a big pill to swallow. Emotions can rise and fall, unpredictably, like a second adolescence.

Dale When the idea of retirement came to mind, I felt like I was on a roller coaster, first euphoric, then terrified. My adventuresome side conjured images of hiking in mountains and river rafting. My cautious side asked me if I wanted to give up what I've been doing for thirty-four years. At times, it was like a tug-of-war and at other times just a mood swing.

A few educators reject the idea of retirement outright in the present and foreseeable future. The loss of purpose and relationships is too great to bear, so they try to "scale down" without quitting. That raises the question of definition.

What does the word *retirement* mean? The best answer is that retirement is in the eye of the beholder although the most frequently referenced definition by educators is this one: Retirement is the formal resignation from one's place of employment after many years of work when one has become eligible for pension payments according to a state plan that usually includes criteria such as age and/or years of service. This definition leaves the door wide open to choices made by the educator once the act of retirement has taken place. Indeed, subsequent choices are so broad and differentially selected that they defy a common definition.

Phillip Retirement in my mind means leaving the world of work completely and moving into a time in life when all my activities are nonwork related.

Grace Changing pace best describes retirement for me. Instead of pushing myself to do everything that I had once done with ease, I pick and choose very deliberately what I do, where I go, and how I choose to spend my energy. It is a boundary marker in life when patterns of behavior are consciously broken.

Markus My conception of retirement has always been related to career and age. In my twenties, I moved into my career of choice; the thirties and forties were midpoints in my career, and the fifties and sixties marked the closing chapter of my full-time career pursuits. It seems to me that retirement is the point where full-time work in one's career is exchanged for a lesser work commitment, usually with another employer, or for a different set of activities for which no monetary payment is made.

Ada Retirement is a reward for working hard and living long. It is permission in the eyes of society to change the first of the two criteria, from working hard to working less time each week, to work but not for money, or to not work, period.

Herbert   Retiring is a watershed time in every person's life when advancing age begins to close some doors and opens others. It is a major life transition. For some educators, the doors close and open with banging and great effort while others seem to go out and in with barely a sound.

MY JOURNEY

The invitation seemed innocent enough. "Would you please present yourself to a distinguished group of educators for possible group membership?" My friend, a retired superintendent, refused to say more. "Trust me," he said. Of course, I went. The eighty-five educators started the evening with dinner, and I surveyed the group intently. All had outstanding reputations in urban education, suburban schools, or tenured university positions. Many were published. Over half were already retired; all the others were on the verge of retiring. After the meal, the group moved to another room, instituted a ritual that enjoined me in some good-natured teasing, and voted unanimously to approve my membership. They flattered me. They honored me. Inadvertently, they also labeled me "soon to be retired." It was a defining moment in my head!

CONCLUSION

The thought of one's own retirement is like the coming of winter. We glance at the calendar but postpone any serious thought and preparation until something subtle, but significant, heightens our sensitivity, like the first frost of fall on the windshield. Sometimes the wake-up call comes as a sharp jab that is thrust at us by a personal confrontation, an unexpected illness, or turn of the tide. This change in life eventually comes to full bore in the mind of every retiree and cannot be deleted or dismissed.

Consciously, one acknowledges retirement as a major, personal crossroad. The line of demarcation becomes fixed in mind, grows over time, and raises the questions of when, how, and what next. The career professional makes this admission to self, and then others: "My time has come. Glory be or heaven help me, a whole new chapter in life is about to be written." Some helpful guidelines follow:

- Tune your ear to hear the first retirement whispers. They are faint, gentle nudges in the direction of one of life's major watersheds.
- Trust your own instincts about retirement; you have honed them over many years. You will face a host of viable options and diverse opinions; you are the ultimate steward of the gift of life.

• Choose a positive attitude toward the coming changes associated with retirement. They are like the incoming tide; they cannot be stopped.
Loosen and extend the anchor lines in your life. Accept and rise to the
forces of time and nature. Ride the waves, see farther, and enjoy the
changing landscape. Otherwise, the sea will always win.

QUESTIONS TO PONDER OR DISCUSS:

1. When did the idea of retirement first enter your mind as a concrete possibility?
2. With whom did you first discuss the possibility of retirement?
3. What was your initial reaction to the idea of retirement?
4. How did your reaction change over time?

CHAPTER TWO

Engaging the Intellect

Most adults begin the retirement journey through the cognitive door. Words are a way of testing the water without actually getting wet. The words change over time from "I will retire someday" to "I will retire soon" to "I will retire this coming June." Each person finds his or her own words and phrases to convey state of mind regarding retirement.

Sherry Beginning at the midpoint in my career, I started talking about retirement. Prompts would come, such as long-term investment decisions, formal letters from the state teacher retirement system, or negotiations about contract language pertaining to severance or retirement. When I talked about my retirement, I always slipped "someday" into the conversation as a kind of safety valve. I wasn't ready to come to grips with the full reality. I knew that once I stated "I will retire soon," the countdown would begin on a whole different plane.

Verbal expression of the prospect of retirement allows exploration of the idea in relative safety. Initially, intellectual exchanges tend to be brief and noncommittal. The conviction to remain or retire grows. Once a "yes" is said to retirement, the intellectual discourse deepens. Thereafter, the words are like the pilings under a bridge that will one day be fully spanned.

Alex My wife said my head works overtime to defend my heart. She reminded me that in our first serious talk about retirement, I stated that retirement is a logical, natural step on the road of life, like infant to child, adolescent to teenager, and college student to professional educator. She claimed, but I don't remember this, I once argued that retirement is simply a new set of clothes, while she argued that retirement is so much more than window dressing.

Rhonda I knew retirement would be a huge change in my life. I held conversations with friends and associates. I sought out people who had moved into what appeared to be well-settled retirement. I participated in seminars, turned to popular magazine articles, and read books. I wanted to be as well prepared for the transition out of my career as I had been in entering it.

MY JOURNEY

I told my wife about the meeting with older, mostly retired educators from around the state, but I kept this thought hidden: My own retirement is in the making. I wasn't yet ready; the words came later following a long school board meeting. Tired, exhausted, and deeply distressed by yet another curriculum controversy, I dragged myself into bed at 11:45 P.M. and sighed, "Retirement is beginning to look more and more appealing, especially if I can do part-time work with less stress." For a long time thereafter, we intellectually tested the idea of retirement in the security of our own home "laboratory" without having to proclaim or defend our findings to anyone else.

CONCLUSION

Words, and lack thereof, can communicate powerfully. For example, many paragraphs of laudatory language within a letter of recommendation are often outweighed by what the writer elected not to mention, which is quickly discerned by experienced human resource directors. The same insight is gleaned from the context and content of conversations pertaining to retirement. Here are some points of discovery:

- How is the topic of retirement introduced? By self or others? By design or happenstance?
- Where are conversations held? Private rooms or busy hallways? Who is included in the group? Close friends or casual acquaintances?
- How long does the conversation last? Passing moment or extended discussion? What tone is reflected in the talk? Lightheartedness or serious probing?
- What parts of speech are evident? First- or third-person pronouns? Verb tenses? Adjectives that signal states of mind and heart?

QUESTIONS TO PONDER OR DISCUSS:

1. What words do you select when you are discussing retirement with someone?
2. How frequently does retirement come up when you converse with other people?
3. In whose company are you discussing retirement?
4. Do you say different things about retirement in varied settings?
5. How imminent or far away is your retirement?

CHAPTER THREE

Handling the Emotional Adjustment

Nearly every retiree reports a powerful emotional component in retirement planning. Initial hesitancy about the retirement idea eventually gives way to acceptance, excitement, and, once in a while, serendipity. That doesn't mean the journey is always smooth.

Karen   The prospect of retirement didn't send me reeling. I assumed if leaving work removed a slice from my psyche, other people and new activities would restore it later. That is exactly what happened.

Megan   The moment I announced my retirement, I felt like a spotlight was beaming on me. Students and parents wished me well. My school planned a reception that turned out to be a huge affair. One sister flew in from California as a special surprise. Poems, songs, and a slide show of my life made us laugh and cry. My husband and I were also given airline tickets to Korea so we could visit our daughter who is teaching English there. I was treated like a queen and finished my career on a tremendous high.

Some retirees report that retirement talk puts their self-esteem under siege. So many aspects of professional life—like occupation, title, assignment, and accomplishment—move from present tense to past tense. The words "I am" become "I was." Relegating professional status to history can cause anxiety about purpose, meaning, and worth to surface.

David   I worried a lot about self-image and self-worth before retirement. So many eggs, so to speak, had been placed in my professional basket. Take that basket away, and what would be left? Thankfully, in the end, my concerns turned out to be groundless. I came to realize that teaching was part of my life, not the whole of it.

Martha   Many of the feelings I had when my husband died from cancer at the age of forty-two came back to me when retirement began to take hold in my mind. I remember thinking that my career was almost like a person and I was saying, "Don't leave me! How can I live without you?" I felt anger but did not know where to direct it. I felt foreboding but could not fully express it.

Expression of one's feelings, whether they are released slowly and deliberately or in a fearful torrent, puts them out where they can be examined more closely. Listeners can play back what they are hearing and raise questions that might lead to personal insight and acceptance of the inevitable.

Vadnais   About midyear during my final year of teaching, I was an emotional wreck. My car needed a jump-start in the cold morning. My mother was in the hospital. My students were hyper. Papers not yet graded had piled up and midterm reports were due for failing students. I was a miserable mess. When my colleague next door popped in after school, I lost it. I just bawled. She gave me a long hug and let me cry. On top of everything else, I had announced my retirement at the start of the school year and wondered if I was premature in this decision. My friend just let me talk and talk until we both noticed the room had become dark with the setting sun.

Vernon   I remember trying to make the call to the personnel director to discuss my retirement. At first I could not find the right time to make the call, and when I finally made the appointment, I nearly canceled it later. My questions centered on the when and how of retiring. I was preoccupied by the steps involved. I did not want to make a major mistake or error that would end my career on an awkward note rather than a positive one. Astutely and with great sensitivity, the director got me to talk about how I was feeling. I began to talk about fears for my health and the stress that had my stomach in knots. I felt much release after our conference. I got a better handle on what to do but, more importantly, I felt someone else I trusted was helping to carry a heavy emotional load.

Educators who are most praised for their dedication, commitment, and service sometimes have the greatest difficulty making the transition into retirement. Rewards, both tangible and intangible, have been tilted toward work rather than other aspects of living.

Dylan   Like my parents on the farm, I followed a dawn-to-dusk work ethic. But, unlike my parents who remained on the farm until their death, I retired from education at age sixty-five and was instantly cut off from my associates, my work, and my routines. I didn't realize how much of my self-worth was tied to school until I retired. Yes, I felt a sense of relief initially, but soon a sense of panic engulfed me. I was like a dry-drunk, not stumbling about but acting out my frustrations with a bad attitude and making life miserable for loved ones around me.

MY JOURNEY

Strong on the outside, soft and vulnerable on the inside, described my emotional state when I went public with my retirement notice. Outwardly, I tried to maintain a calm, business-as-usual composure, while inwardly my emotions were on edge. Was September the right time of year to make the announcement? What would happen to loyal colleagues and key initiatives under a new administration? Would other opportunities come along to help pay the bills for five to ten years? How did I tactfully convey that I still wanted and needed to work when work associates and citizens might assume a full, complete retirement?

On Friday nights, my wife and I drove for four hours to our lake place where we worked feverishly on remodeling projects, releasing tensions and seeing a tangible product unfold, while professionally things were in flux. On Sundays, our long trip back to the city included extended periods of silence mingled with talk and prayers about future possibilities, our hopes, and sources of help as well as our doubts and fears.

CONCLUSION

Educators should not deny or trample upon whatever emotions arise on the retirement journey. Emotions are nature's way of helping with transition: expose the furies who always are companions of change, provide the warning signs when caution is appropriately indicated, and seek out protective angels who can illuminate dark corners and paint bold, bright pictures of the future. They provide the energy to act decisively and proactively when conditions are suited for navigation through new waters. Powerful emotions sustain the marathon runners in education, enabling them to cross the retirement finish line. Additionally, they help retirees prepare for the next big race called the second half of life. Some tips for training follow:

- Attach words to feelings and emotions that are associated with your retirement.
- Express to loving friends and family your fears, hopes, sorrows, joys, doubts, and whatever else comes to mind about retirement.

- Seek out others who care about you, are more objective than you, or know about retirement firsthand.
- Encourage trusted advisors to give feedback about what they are seeing and hearing, raise insightful questions, and provide the comfort of friendship and a sense of belonging through this period of profound change.

QUESTIONS TO PONDER OR DISCUSS:

1. Describe your emotional reaction(s) when you first considered retirement.
2. Has your self-esteem been tested by pending retirement? If so, how?
3. What retirement prospects give rise to pleasant feelings? What retirement issues and concerns are troubling, possibly even disturbing, your peace of mind or sleep habits?
4. With whom can you discuss your innermost feelings about pending retirement?
5. How are you feeling as the day of retirement approaches?
6. What major day-to-day goals will seem like a loss? What will replace them?

CHAPTER FOUR

Anticipating Behavior Anomalies

Many retirees report that the advent of retirement prompts behavioral changes that fall outside of those occasioned by lame-duck status. Some behaviors are very much out of character.

Fred   When school started, I said it would be my last year and wanted to go out on a high. Midyear, I had a wake-up call from my department chair. He said I talked less, was withdrawn, and no longer showed my old enthusiasm for curriculum projects and special events like homecoming. He urged me not to retire in spirit until I retired in fact. Looking back, I think I was depressed. I had stopped pushing to do and be better, didn't like the new me, and began to falter.

June   I'm am energetic person; people have told me this all my life. I have never lacked energy to do things, go places, and be actively engaged. I am a strong committee person, pursue projects with vigor, go to work with bounce in my step, and greet others with open arms. When the prospect of retirement first struck me, I found myself losing energy. The sun didn't look as bright in the morning or feel as warm. My lesson plans waited until the last minute. I missed committee meetings. I was more edgy with students. My weight decreased. I felt like a Raggedy Ann doll. My friends began to ask me if I was O.K.

Serious retirement talk can touch the nerve center of one's life. All that which has gone on before, the good and the bad, and all that has not occurred but was part of a professional dream can rise to the surface of consciousness.

Jeff   Dad was already a school superintendent in a small town when I was growing up. It was a good life and I entered teaching without much thought about other career choices. Quietly in my heart, however, I carried the goal of becoming an administrator like my father, only in a large suburban setting. It was not to be. Marriage and children came early. My first teaching job was far from a college so taking graduate classes was a hardship both on time with my family and the pocketbook. I never got into administration. Sometimes I think I was lucky. Other times I wonder what might have been.

Pending retirement can be like opening a history book that is written in one's own handwriting. The pages are filled with memories of old relationships: friends whose whereabouts are not known and others who are still everyday companions, people who did injury or who failed to hold a trust, and associates who created opportunities or put up roadblocks. Happy memories cheer like blooming flowers while sad memories discourage like garden weeds.

Kelly   My first flashback was in the car after the fall curriculum night for students and parents. On the way home I noted to myself, "I will not be giving a pep talk like that ever again." Like an instant rerun, I saw Mrs. Williams, my middle school math teacher, standing in the classroom pounding home her conviction that girls are able to learn math, until I finally believed her. Then my mind switched back to the present. Would any of my students ever bring me to mind? How will I be remembered?

Ronald   A board member voted "no" on a proposal the same night I announced my retirement as school superintendent. I had wanted this to be a perfect meeting with little or no dissension. It was not to be. My mind flipped me back twenty years when a "no" vote by a single board member on a referendum proposal became the rallying cry for the opposition. The ensuing defeat forced my resignation and prompted a move to a new school district. That was a bitter pill to swallow at the time and still gives me indigestion now and then.

Educators are masters of change in others, but this does not always translate back to readiness for change in self. We often see the splinter in the eye of others before we acknowledge the beam in our own eye. Sometimes, the beam is held in place by ego, high job satisfaction, or the false sense of prestige in being the last to retire. The wall of resistance then becomes a type of handicap as retirement approaches.

George   For a long, long time, I resisted the idea of retirement even when my wife and school superintendent expressed concerns about my health. I watched each grade level move through the system like waves on the shoreline. As a teacher, then principal, I encouraged and exhorted these young people all along the way and watched with rightful pride when they graduated. Graduates returned with success stories. They rewarded and reinforced my life purposes. I knew I was growing older, of course, but leaving all this behind did not compute in my brain as a positive choice until chest pains one night led to bypass surgery and a complete overhaul in my short- and long-range thinking.

Sally   I played school as a child. I knew I wanted to be a teacher since elementary school. My early dreams became my career's delight. I loved teaching kindergarten. When my own children were born, I switched to nursery school children so I could spend more time at home. My husband was ready for retirement at the age of sixty when he resigned from his position as principal, but I was not. I continued to teach another five years until getting down and up from the floor with small children became very hard for me. Now my legs seriously bother me when I walk and limit the trips we can take as a couple. I should have retired earlier.

Retirement often prompts changes in people close to the retiree—words spoken, deeds done, and reactions shown. Likewise, one's own behaviors are put under the microscope like an out-of-body observer who wants to gain new perspective on how one's retirement transition is coming along. Everything seems overlaid with added emotional charges. The electrical surges bring old practices into question and new options into sharper view.

Dennis   These thoughts crossed my mind dozens of times: What is going on here? What is happening to me? My lesson plans from last year, the year before that, and going back even further were much the same. Normally, I would dust them off, polish them up, and be ready to go without much extra work or great inspiration. In my last year of teaching, I poured my heart and soul into those lesson plans. Sometimes I tried new instructional techniques, a kind of risk-taking behavior. It was as though I wanted to experiment one last time. Sometimes I selected unfamiliar materials for classes that required extra reading and preparation on my part. Maybe I was practicing for the new and unexpected after retirement. In any case, my final year was filled with a creativity that I had not felt since I began my teaching career, and I felt an extra burst of energy like a runner approaching the finish line.

Pamela   Normally, I take most everything in stride with few self-doubts before or after events. This changed in the weeks prior to my last day of work. I found myself going to events, especially retirement functions, with something like pregame jitters for starting players. Questions surfaced: How do I look? Who will be there watching me? Will my nervousness show? Will my tight muscles relax? How will I perform? Who can I count on? Can I get through this without making a mistake? Why am I here in the first place?

MY JOURNEY

As far as I know, few of my outward behaviors changed after announcing my retirement. However, some private behaviors belied significant stress. I spent more time away from people, safely distanced from well-wishers and inquirers about future plans. Instead of rushing in my car from one school to another, I drove slower, sometimes taking a more scenic route. This delayed my arrival to schools where, historically, I had hurried and relished every visit. Writing editorials, drafting speeches, and preparing agendas became more of a struggle. My mind wandered and lost focus more easily. More of my time and attention shifted to what comes next in my life. My caring didn't lessen, just my ability to respond, create, and motivate myself to produce at the highest levels.

CONCLUSION

All educators who live long lives retire, eventually. For some, their passage models balking, sulking, or even rebellious behavior, much like that put to verse by poet Dylan Thomas.[*] His title, also the first line, sets the tone, and the two subsequent lines predicate behavior anomalies.

> Do not go gentle into that good night,
> Old age should burn and rave at close of day;
> Rage, rage against the dying of the light.

Awkward and occasional outrageous moments on the road to retirement do pass. Atypical behaviors observed by colleagues and family members are readily understood, accepted, excused, forgiven, and forgotten. Outwardly, most retiring persons continue to act quite normally, consistent with their personality, although self-perceptions may judge otherwise. According to conversations with 300 retirees, the following preretirement behaviors fall within the normal range:

- Routines command fuller attention again, moving back to stick shift after years on automatic drive.
- Patterns change, like high school seniors from February to June: avoiding some individuals and situations, seeking out special people with whom to talk, and going to typical school events with melancholy, or gladness that they can soon be crossed off the list.

---

[*] Dylan Thomas, "Do Not Go Gentle into That Good Night," *The Poems of Dylan Thomas* (New York: New Directions, 1971).

- All of the following, with slight exaggerations, may occur: talking more or less, frowning inside and smiling outside, sleeping better or worse, feeling up or down, and seeing new connections or feeling like you lost your place in a musical score.
- Tensions rise higher, last longer, and accelerate or, conversely, a peaceful spirit floods the heart.
- Periods of high, even intense, productivity are followed by down times when energy flags and projects lag.
- Time awareness increases. It can evaporate faster than ever and, alternately, drag like never before.
- Professional pride prompts diligence, although occasional slippages in performance may be evident on lesser matters.
- Illness may increase, especially if nerves are frayed and exhaustion consumes.
- Nostalgia reigns supreme, often triggered by seemingly unrelated things.
- Tasks done for the last time prompt reflection, and mixed feelings float like billowing clouds in the sky.

QUESTIONS TO PONDER OR DISCUSS:

1. What is happening to your energy level since the start of serious retirement talk?
2. What personal behaviors, if any, do you discern have changed since you decided to retire?
3. Has anyone questioned how you are handling this retirement business? If so, was it casual conversation or a probing inquiry into changed behavior? Who initiated it?
4. Does pending retirement give rise to career flashbacks? If so, describe them.
5. What will you miss most about ending your career?
6. What regrets, if any, come to mind as you consider retirement?

CHAPTER FIVE

Identifying Immediate Issues and Concerns

Very practical matters move to primary consideration when the possibility of retirement moves beyond the stage of casual conversation to serious exploration. Educators often name finance their number one concern. (Section III will address, in depth, four major challenges in retirement: finance, residences, relationships, and health.)

David   Can I afford to retire? This was my foremost question. The month-to-month paycheck from the school district would end. Would my state pension payment become less, stay the same, or increase? Investigating this question became my top priority.

Nancy   My husband died young. I invested the life insurance money. I had stayed home for a number of years to raise my children, which meant I was not eligible for maximum teacher retirement benefits. Would I need a part-time job following retirement to pay my bills, or would the combination of state pension and portfolio performance meet my needs? These were key questions for me.

Wesley   The income side of my retirement budget was fairly easy to determine. However, the expense side of the ledger was another thing. Paychecks had been covering our expenses so neither my wife nor I balanced our checkbooks carefully, nor had we been doing serious analysis of our annual expenses. Digging into our check register and Visa bills would help provide data on past practices, but what expense assumptions should be used for retirement years? Would our expenses go up, down, or stay the same? These critical questions bothered me.

Another related concern frequently expressed by retirees centers on health. The threat of accident, illness, or life-destroying disease is taken more personally. Also, older persons are especially wary of rising health insurance costs and express anxiety about the quality of health care.

Gene   So many insurance questions flooded my mind. I knew Medicare coverage becomes available at age sixty-five, but what about the five years before I reached that age? Would I be eligible for school health insurance if I retired before age sixty-five? My list of questions grew by the day.

Ann   During all my working years, I was uneasy about selecting a health program from the many offered through our district. I depended heavily upon choices made by my colleagues. My anxiety grew with approaching retirement because I knew my colleagues and I would soon be going our separate ways. Who would help me then?

Harold   A dentist friend moved to Colorado and complained that doctor after doctor there refused to accept new patients covered by Medicare. My wife and I wanted to travel after retirement and perhaps settle in another state. My friend's personal experience made me leery. How could I be sure of good health care and health insurance coverage in other states before making a move?

Sylvia   My husband was self-employed. My school health insurance policy provided his medical coverage during my working years. He and I wondered about medical insurance after I retired. Would school insurance cover only me, both of us, or neither of us? Would I be eligible for supplemental insurance through the school district when I turned sixty-five? How about my husband? Questions like these dominated our thinking until we got solid answers.

Utilizing hours once spent in school-related work is another concern of educators who anticipate their retirement. However, the topic of scheduling is seldom mentioned by educators after one year of retirement, except to observe that every minute is filled, and to question if a harried schedule equates with the wise use of time.

Joel   I about went nuts in the weeks prior to my retirement. Friends, associates, neighbors, and even family members asked me repeatedly what I was going to do in retirement. Honestly, I did not know but to say "I don't know," which created an awkward pause in the conversation and left me feeling empty and somewhat guilty that I was somewhat at sea how best to spend my retirement time.

Mariana   The first few months after retirement I would run into people who knew me during my working years. I could predict their first two questions without fail: 1) How are you? 2) What are you doing these days? The truth was, I was still exploring options, testing ideas, and seeking answers. The questions seemed to imply that all these things should be sorted out and that I should have a laundry list of new activities ready to recite.

Cindy   How did I find time to work all those years? My daily schedule is filled to the brim. No two days are alike. When my friends and I get some notion to go someplace or do something, we get off our duff and do it. I'm beginning to do some soul searching whether this is the best way to spend my time.

Nicholas   My lifestyle changed completely after I had a stroke. I can get around with a walker, but I walk so slowly. Hours are now gobbled up just getting from here to there. Golf and tennis are out of the question. More sedentary activities fill the gap.

MY JOURNEY

Once a year, over the past two decades, I have updated our family's financial records to obtain a good handle on our family's net worth. The spreadsheets showed all sources of income and categories of expenditures. Typically, it was a testy time around our house. Some of my wife's checks did not indicate for what the money was spent and my asking may have sounded more like an inquisition than an inquiry. In any case, from one year to the next, a fairly accurate record accumulated, allowing for good trend analysis. In my last year of full-time work, I added the numbers up repeatedly, changed assumptions, and added the figures all over again. It was almost like a compulsion. I had a best case, worst case, and most likely case scenario for the years following retirement, each providing financial targets on the income and expense side of the ledger.

CONCLUSION

Survival instincts take hold when the reality of retirement sinks into the mind and heart. Most educators have enough self-confidence and common sense to realize they can get through the upcoming life challenges because millions of retired educators have obviously gone this way before.

However, retirees are like new patrons in a strange restaurant, asking "How much does this cost?" "What do most people like best?" "What do you recommend?" No question surrounding retirement is out of line. Many inquiries flow from points of vulnerability and insecurity that must be addressed to achieve peace of mind. Rational decision making begins with honest exploration. Practical matters like those below need to be addressed:

- Present income, future income, best and worst case projections.
- Present expenses, future expenses, best and worst case projections.
- Financial impact of retiring right away versus working one or two more years.
- Present and future health coverage for self and any other dependents.
- Readiness for retirement, mentally and emotionally.
- Timeline for decision making.
- Projects, events, assignments that should be finished.
- Available experts on all questions.
- Next-step plans following retirement.

QUESTIONS TO PONDER OR DISCUSS:

1. To what extent have you planned for retirement, financially? What are current and future income and expense projections? What debts are outstanding? What are the best and worst case scenarios in each instance?
2. What changes in retirement do you anticipate in health insurance coverage and how will premiums be paid? Will travel or change of residence have an impact?
3. What is your motivation to retire? What else do you need to know to put conviction into your decision and feel comfortable with it?
4. What is the minimum that you must do to feel good and ready about leaving your present position? What remaining projects, tasks, and assignments must be completed?
5. To whom can you turn for help with these practical matters pertaining to finance and a smooth transition for yourself and others?

CHAPTER SIX

Formalizing the Act of Retirement

Most educators report the importance of consulting with others before making the decision to retire. The list of confidants and advisors is extensive: family members, valued friends, trusted colleagues, long-term mentors, work supervisors, and state retirement counselors.

Carmon   I wanted an expert opinion about the state's retirement plan. Loose talk around the faculty lounge wasn't good enough for an important decision like this. I made an appointment with a state official.

Dawn   My sister and I talked about possible retirement for many months before I resigned. She is a good listener and keeps confidences, absolutely.

Arthur   I called my long-time mentor, a retired superintendent, about my retirement plans. The rumor mill hums at the slightest provocation. I did not want a "lame-duck" situation before its time.

Ann Elise   My principal was there for me when my father died and when I went through a messy divorce. I was comfortable turning to him yet a third time when I needed help with the pros and cons of early retirement.

Andrew   I spoke with no one other than my wife, thinking this was a personal and family decision more than a professional one.

Mary Jo   Everyone within earshot heard me discuss the retirement possibilities. I watched their faces intently, gauged their reactions, and got some good advice, too.

The act of retirement requires a formal, written notice. Orally stating one's intentions puts everyone into the alert mode, but only a written statement meets the legal requirement. The resignation letter can be as simple as this: "I hereby resign effective . . ." followed with one's signature and date. It can also be a multipage resignation letter citing career highlights and expressing appreciation all around. On occasion, a supervisor will provide a form letter to expedite an immediate resignation.

Amy   I loved teaching and would have liked to continue, but my husband had retired earlier and wished to travel during the school year. Writing my resignation letter was a huge step for me. I referenced mentors over the years, the joys of working with children, and my gratitude for parent and community support. The letter was very long and provided a much-needed catharsis. I heard many of my own words read aloud at the retirement dinner sponsored by the school board.

Chris   My last years of teaching wore me out. Literally, I was burned out. I decided to resign after the school year ended and then to disappear from the school scene without fanfare. I wrote out a two-line resignation notice, signed it, and mailed it to the central office.

Verdi   Two paragraphs comprised my resignation letter. In one I noted how long I had worked in the district and what a pleasure it had been. In the other I expressed my best wishes to those who would carry on.

When is the right time to make the retirement announcement? Most educators give advance oral notice several months before the actual date of retirement and submit the formal letter of resignation a month or two before school term ends. Some state laws or local teacher contracts specify a date by which the retirement notification must be submitted to be effective, usually the end of the school calendar year. However, requests to resign after that date are usually granted because the prospect of forcing someone to work who wants to retire puts the organization at risk. Earlier resignations are helpful in two respects: (1) allowing sufficient time to recruit, select, and hire a replacement and (2) allowing time for a gracious farewell.

Joyce   Finding the right replacement sometimes takes a long time, so I submitted my resignation letter in early spring. We have a strong science department and I wanted to do everything possible to keep it that way.

Paul   The history in this district is to conduct a national search for a school superintendent whenever a vacancy occurs. The whole process consumes months of time if well done. Although I did not relish a long "lame-duck" status, I announced my retirement nine months prior to my last day of work.

Samuel   I left my teaching post after thirty-four years. I hadn't intended to leave the way I did—a rather abrupt resignation in late June. It was too late for any, "We're sorry to see you go and here's your tin cup" comments. The decision was prompted by a belated visit with a counselor from the state retirement association who showed me that my pension would be 95 percent of my teaching salary, plus I was promised generous yearly increases. And, if I looked more critically and honestly, I was a bit bored with the whole scene. I was beginning to repeat myself in classes year after year.

Personal choice is also involved regarding to whom the retirement letter is sent. Addressing the letter to the person in the administration who knows you the best can provide emotional support in this major life transition. In the end, the board of education takes the legal step of accepting the resignation to make it official.

Margaret   All communications to the central office go through the principal so I put his name on my letter of resignation.

Marty   My retirement letter was addressed to the chairperson of the school board. We have had a respectful working relationship, and it seemed right as superintendent to address it to her with copies to the other board members.

Brad   I've known the personnel director for years. We used to teach in rooms side by side. I put his name on my letter of resignation to acknowledge our special relationship.

Patrick   I won't go into details, but I was pressured to resign. The form resignation letter the principal gave me to sign said "To Whom It May Concern."

Carol   I made the decision to resign after talking to my department chair. Shortly thereafter I composed my resignation letter. I addressed it to the superintendent, but I hand-delivered it to my department head out of respect for her leadership, guidance, and friendship for so many years.

MY JOURNEY

One of many jobs for a school superintendent is to put out little fires before they become a firestorm. Having served as the "chief fireman" for twenty-four years in the same district, I was proud of the district's record of outstanding accomplishments, but I was also aware of scar tissue I had accumulated in the process. Talking it through with the board of education, a joint decision was made that the time was right for a new, unmarked leader. The parting was harmonious and, indeed, mutually supportive.

The retirement parties were numerous and well attended. The gift giving by friends, associates, and residents was generous; all money (thousands of dollars) went to the school foundation for excellence in teaching and learning. My resignation letter, about two pages long and submitted in September, went to the school board chair and was read into the public record, citing the many strengths in the district, pinpointing things needing special attention, and wishing the board, staff, students, citizens, and eventual replacement my best wishes. I continued to serve full time for the next nine months. No bridges were burned and good relations exist to this day.

CONCLUSION

The professional ideal for educators is hand shaking at the time of employment and hand clapping at the time of resignation. To this end, some points of protocol are suggested:

- Talk through retirement possibilities with someone who knows you well, such as a friend or family member, because he or she has your best interests at heart.
- Communicate privately with a trusted supervisor regarding your retirement intentions, although a formal public announcement may not occur for some time.
- Explore your retirement questions with colleagues and trusted advisors. Your inquiries are a form of honor, and through this, they will become good partners on this walk.
- Formally announce your retirement so that sufficient time remains to recruit and fill the vacancy and to plan farewell events without being hurried.
- Write a letter of resignation that fits your personality, conveys your positive sentiments, refrains from hurting others, and emphasizes sincerity.
- At retirement functions, go out in style: dress appropriately, listen attentively, and speak graciously. Laugh, cry, patiently hear stories, and bravely tell appropriate stories. Remember always that the loving and grieving rituals are to help you and your associates through this transitional time.
- Return the kindnesses that are extended to you with notes of appreciation. Such professional and personal courtesy will strengthen friend-

ships, encourage others, and yield goodwill that is most helpful for references during retirement years.

QUESTIONS TO PONDER OR DISCUSS:

1. What factors do you think are a consideration in choosing people with whom to discuss retirement possibilities?
2. What time of year do you plan to announce your intention to retire? When do you plan to submit your formal retirement letter? What rationale lies behind this timing?
3. What do you plan to include as content within your retirement letter? Why?
4. To whom will your retirement letter be addressed? Why?
5. To what extent do you plan to participate in retirement activities?
6. What perspective will you bring to retirement events?

SCANNING POSTRETIREMENT POSSIBILITIES

The front porch rocker is an old-fashioned image for the modern day retiree. Many educators retire when they are less than sixty-five years of age. Indeed, some become eligible for retirement in their middle to late fifties. At the same time, projections of a life span continue to push outward. Educators find that their energy levels are still high and that most friends in noneducational fields are still working full time. These are reminders that the work ethic abounds.

The range of options available to educators in retirement is wider and deeper than first imagined. Simply "filling hours" once consumed by career pursuits is a narrow and shallow perspective. Scanning postretirement possibilities must encompass not only former work hours but the whole of life. By default or by design, every retiree eventually answers questions relating to the future. Identifying and analyzing all the possibilities, of course, come first. This soul searching (described in chapter 7) leads eventually to personal preferences among innumerable choices.

Retirement activities of educators fall into four major categories. Chapter 8 notes individual interests mentioned by many retirees. Chapter 9 identifies part-time educational choices that bring satisfaction to those who elect to remain in the school environment. Chapter 10 describes the range of part-time to full-time employment possibilities within both the private and for profit sectors. Chapter 11 explores public service options that provide fulfillment to many newly retired educators.

The intent in section II is not to catalog every postretirement possibility—an impossible task—but to prime the pump. What is right for one person can be totally wrong for another. Nearly all retirees, however, report that choices made at the onset of retirement are reassessed again and again. What may seem ideal in early stages of retirement may not feel right or be right at a subsequent date. Retirement is a transition that continues for the whole of life.

CHAPTER SEVEN

Exploring Choices with New Freedom

Retirement opens huge blocks of time that once were highly scheduled in work-related activities. Like a sunrise that gradually illuminates the new day, the retiree begins to see possibilities, some not visible before and others not fully considered. Clearly, the responsibilities, routines, and rigor of professional work have ended. An entirely new season in life has begun.

Anne When I was growing up, I often sat on the potty for a long time so I spent the time daydreaming. My visions nearly always took me into the future where I could see myself studying, graduating, teaching, marrying, raising kids, buying a house, and living a very full life. At age sixty-five, I still sit on the john for extended periods and daydream. However, I no longer have clear images about future activities, events, hopes, and dreams. I am not unhappy or depressed—just less certain about what could, should, or will come next in my life.

Educators often report that retirement held the image of doing things not possible while working full time. Inactivity was the last thing in their minds.

Lauren When I retired, I never once considered doing nothing. Sitting around was the last thing on my agenda. Travel brochures flooded my mailbox. Elderhostel programs intrigued me. TV advertisements recruited older workers for fast-food restaurants like McDonalds. Former colleagues accepted part-time positions in education. Invitations came to volunteer in organizations. Card-playing friends asked me to join their bridge group. I had a stack of books to read and my children insisted I come for a visit. I wanted to do it all.

The cultural norm for retirees in twenty-first-century America is to be busy doing something. Gambone (2000) captures this theme in his book *ReFirement: A Boomer's Guide to Life after Fifty.* The persistent question for the retiree, whether asked of self or by others, is this: "What is next for me on the road of life?" For some, the answers come quickly and easily. Others need time to sort out possibilities.

Kermit   I just wanted to get away. Away from the job . . . away from neighbors . . . away from questions about my future plans . . . just away. A month-long tour around the Mediterranean Sea aboard a cruise ship sounded just right. Old cities en route sparked my interest as I'd been a history major, and I envisioned my mental, emotional, and physical overload going overboard as I sat in a sun-drenched deck chair with beautiful, blue water on every horizon. What I really needed was to regain a sense of equilibrium. My hope was that some time away from everything and everyone would help clear my head and allow the sorting out process to begin.

The bane and blessing for a newly retired educator is life with a blank sheet. The working world of the past has been erased in one stroke of the pen. What activities will fill that void can generate excitement and delight, anxiety and depression, or both in alternating mood swings. The resulting introspection and investigation reveal life's issues that go far beyond the replacement of the school day with alternative activities.

Sophia   Initially, my husband and I thought our retirement challenge would center on how to fill the hours that had previously been spent in school. True, this single concern was the starting point, but it soon expanded to reach every aspect of our lives as a couple, like the layers of an onion. We grossly underestimated the breadth of issues to be addressed and the fact that every aspect of our living would also come under the microscope. For example, do we continue to live in the same house, same community, or even the same state? Given the change in our annual income, do we change the size and focus of our annual charitable gifts? What organizational memberships, magazine subscriptions, and volunteer activities should we add or delete? The list goes on and on.

Quite common to educators writing their resignation letter is this fundamental question: Should I retire? Of course, this question is not new at this point, but the full reality of retirement comes to a head in facing the blank sheet of paper and making the legal commitment. Related thoughts often arise: I don't have to leave. No state or federal law forces me to resign. My long seniority protects me from budgetary cutbacks. Incentives for retirement are not obligations, only inducements, and they may be offered again at some later date. Thus, the first personal option is whether or not to retire early.

Linda   Our state legislature made a one-time exception in the retirement rules for educators. The Rule of 90 became Rule of 85: age, plus experience, adding up to 85. I weighed it carefully. However, I found myself saying that all those postretirement questions can wait. I was a good teacher and still loved to work with kids. Why hurry into an uncertain future when the present is so satisfying, personally and professionally?

Curt   Having served as a building principal for many years, veteran staff members frequently talked with me about their retirement, especially as the end of the school year loomed. If the staff member seemed happy in his or her work, I did not encourage early retirement. The last years of teaching can become the most productive of an entire career. Our children are raised, the nest is empty, parents have either passed away or are not yet in need of extra care, and one's full energy and focus can be brought to bear on youth and their instruction. I can name a dozen educators who told me after the fact that they retired too early.

One commonality among retirees is an in-depth assessment of life issues and related decisions that cover a much wider range than had come to mind initially. Some options are like small crossroads that are barely noticeable to a person driving a fast-moving vehicle, whereas other options are like formidable bridges that move the driver into a whole new territory. The absolute reality is that every educator will become a retirement road warrior. Some study maps carefully and advance cautiously. Others venture forth with little more than gas in the tank and minimal concern for the new and unexpected.

Heather   I did my homework. I knew retirement would be a huge change in my life and I wanted to prepare myself as much as possible. I held conversations with friends and associates of similar ages. I sought out people who had moved into what appeared to be well-settled retirement. I made lists of questions and answers that flowed from these contacts. I attended retirement seminars, turned to popular magazine articles, and read books. I had spent four years in college to earn my teaching degree. Not to focus conscientiously on the next chapter in my life seemed downright foolish.

Allison   I was programmed from morning to night during all my working years. I did not hate or resent the crowded calendar and busy days. However, in retirement I wanted more serendipity. I wanted more spontaneity in my life. That old cowboy song "Don't Fence Me In" captures my spirit these days.

Robert   The book Managing Transitions: Making the Most of Change (1991) by William Bridges became a valuable resource for the school board, principals, my wife, and me in the months before my retirement as a superintendent. It seemed that everyone who retired said to us how busy they were, and we wanted less to be busy than to put our time and energy into the best possible uses. One Bible verse that became a beacon light to us was I Samuel 9:27: "Stop here yourself for awhile, that I may make known to you the word of God." We determined not to reprogram ourselves immediately, but to sort out what was critically important from that which was interesting and simply time filling.

MY JOURNEY

I took note of two lawyer friends who retired ahead of me. Like me, they had worked long hours each week, but they did not suddenly close up their practice. They accepted fewer clients, reduced their hours of work, and eased into retirement. It was like a gradual, controlled retirement. That made good sense to me—clearly a healthy choice. I started thinking how a school administrator could retire and work part-time. Educational consulting got the nod. I began to take inventory: What did I like to do? What could I do well? What results could I cite to prove my competence? Which of these things could I do alone, not wanting to be encumbered by partners, bureaucracy, or administrative overhead?"

CONCLUSION

Once retirement occurs, the next steps include the "taking of stock." Earlier speculation of possibilities gives way to the reality that choices must now be made. This process goes down two distinct roads but results in a unified goal: (1) outward, to identify choices that are available to retired educators in the immediate and larger world and, (2) inward, to uncover or discover one's interests, abilities, needs, desires, and dreams that are waiting to be pursued and realized. Solid matches materialize when the results of personal assessment are overlaid on possibilities. This outward and inward inventory should be a conscious, deliberate undertaking. Otherwise, all possibilities look good, focus is lost, and a pattern can develop of being busy all the time without a true sense of fulfillment. Some helpful suggestions follow:

- Seek out persons who retired earlier to glean from their experiences about choices, challenges, and commitments in postretirement years.
- Read books that describe postretirement possibilities that others have incorporated into their lives. (A starting-point bibliography is included at the end of this book.)

EXPLORING CHOICES WITH NEW FREEDOM   37

- Talk to family members who know you well and other colleagues who have worked with you to hear what they think about possible postretirement matches.
- Go away, withdraw, retreat, and otherwise separate yourself. Allow introspection to go deep, proceed without interruption, and be very honest. What is truly important to me? What do I want to do and accomplish? Who do I want to become? And what business is unfinished that could cause regrets at the end of my life?

QUESTIONS TO PONDER OR DISCUSS:

1. What postretirement activities come first to mind when you contemplate retirement?
2. What types of activities are you currently engaged in that you wish to continue in retirement?
3. What major factors do you think should be considered when deciding activities to pursue in retirement?
4. What retirement activities do you anticipate will bring you the most pleasure, satisfaction, and fulfillment? Why?
5. With whom can you discuss postretirement possibilities?
6. What, if anything, is holding up your introspection of self relative to postretirement possibilities? How do you plan to eliminate these roadblocks?

CHAPTER EIGHT

Pursuing Individual Interests

Educators, especially those new to retirement, report finding pleasure in small things. Personal interests and desires, once restricted, now can be unleashed. Pent-up energy flows unchecked by clocks, lesson plans, meeting schedules, and obligations related to professional responsibilities.

Kathy This may sound trivial, but the most immediate and dramatic change for me was not being sleep deprived any more. It took over a month, but I feel like a different person.

Mark My wife and I finally cleaned out the garage and basement storage room. It's like a monkey off our backs.

Betsy I brought my travel scrapbooks up to date. Bits and pieces had been lying around for years.

Rebecca Luxurious baths, sometimes twice a day, were heavenly; I mellowed out.

Boyd Finally, I was able to work out at the health club without getting up at the crack of dawn.

Kerry What a pleasure—read the whole newspaper over morning coffee!

Marne My stack of "must-read" books quickly dwindled. I've read more books in the first three months of retirement than in the previous ten years.

Bruce I loved mowing my lawn in the middle of the day.

Barb The first time in our lives my husband and I saw all the movies up for academy awards, and here is the best part—we saw most of them during afternoon hours.

Hobbies are an important activity for most educators. Retirement permits pursuit of such activities without any interference from professional duties. Like nectar for the honeybee, hobbies can feed and nourish passions and give expression to innate abilities.

Tom   My hobby is oil painting. I like to find beautiful landscapes and transfer the scenes to canvases. All the pressures of life leave me when I look for an ideal setting to paint and become absorbed in capturing the colors and beauty I see in my mind. My hobby requires extended periods of time to do my best work, so fortunately retirement has been a boon for my hobby. Elongated time blocks are available to me day after day.

Mary   I love to play the piano. I'm not a professional, but I can and do play both popular and classical music. Tensions of the day lessen as my fingers ply the keys. When I play familiar pieces, my heart fairly sings and prayers of thanksgiving for music and life go from me to God. I relished the day when I could play and play, unfettered by long hours spent at school. Retirement has given me the freedom to play piano as often and as long as I want. Praise the Lord!

Leo   Athletics have been prominent in my life, first as an athlete, then as a coach. In these latter years, golf has become my hobby. I have a membership at the country club but, in the past, had been frustrated by crowded tee times after school and on weekends. Now, in retirement, my buddies and I can play during the day several days a week. About five years ago, our city developed a nine-hole course on what had been the grounds for an old TB sanitarium; it is located just five blocks east of our home. If our family schedule is fairly full for a day, I can often get in a quick round before or after other activities. If there is such as thing as reincarnation, I'd like to come back as a golf pro.

Ross   I taught secondary students how to work with wood. I still love the smell of wood and have my own woodshop at the lake cabin. I carve wooden ducks and geese. Every year I donate some pieces to charity auctions and church fundraising events. I like the thought that some worthwhile causes are receiving a much needed boost and that people are enjoying my waterfowl carvings in their homes.

Pius   I have just one lament: I don't have enough time to do all I want.

Unless personal interests and hobbies are already present in the educator's life, the transition into retirement can pose more of a challenge. Many retirees report such a challenge, because the demands of their professional positions or their devotion to work consumed all available hours. Those who discover their latent interests and special abilities following retirement are at a very different starting point than those who retire with a wide range of interests already well established.

Caleb   When the school board informed me privately at age sixty-two that they would not renew my superintendent's contract for another three years, I decided it was my time to retire. I quietly announced my retirement to save face. At first, I deeply missed the programmed nature of my professional day, the intensity of relationships often in conflict, and the sense of importance attached to every task. I found myself waking up at the same early hour every day only to discover nothing was in place for me to do. Gradually, I began to feel adrenaline withdrawal and a kind of lethargy set in that left me feeling impotent and rather worthless. I had very little practice being alone, much less doing things that brought personal pleasure and relaxation. In fact, I had to rediscover who I was deep inside of me and this process was more than a bit painful and humbling.

Interests may lay dormant for most of one's life, then spring into being with a surprising release of energy at the advent of retirement. Retirees frequently name travel, exercise, and lifelong learning activities.

Phyllis   During my working years, my husband's work kept him on a short leash, so we only traveled within the USA. Since his death and my retirement, I've been to South Africa, India, Russia, Argentina, and the Philippines. Sometimes I travel with group tours and at other times with friends. Here is an excerpt from one of my e-mails: "Wow! What an adventure the past two weeks . . . Moscow, Yaroslavl, Yekaterinburg, and Irkutsk on the Trans-Siberian Rail. Tuesday we visited Lake Baikal, the world's deepest lake. All the water of the five Great Lakes wouldn't fill it. We had an omul (fish) dinner; this fish lives only in Lake Baikal."

Dylan   Our goal is to ride our bicycles in every state of the union. We are a little over halfway there. About the time of our retirement, a doctor recommended more exercise. Little did we realize that riding the bike trails near our home would catapult us to adventures all over the country.

Ruth   Never once during my working years did I take a class provided through the community education program of our school district. I was too busy. Retirement opened big spaces in my life and the catalog of courses that

I had been discarding for years and years caught my attention. Night classes are now a delightful time in my life and I tell other retirees to join me in the fun.

MY JOURNEY

I consciously broke long-established life patterns. At first, I slept in a little longer—well, maybe an "extra" hour. I read the paper each morning from cover to cover while eating my cereal. Symbolically, I broke my rule of reading just one book at a time. We expanded weekends at the cabin from three days to four or five. I did more babysitting of the youngest grandchild. I converted a storeroom under a three-season porch into a hobby shop. I installed and learned some computer programs that had long interested me. We sold our old bicycles in a garage sale and purchased new ones with front-wheel shock absorbers.

CONCLUSION

Many educators know how to spoil grandchildren. Following retirement, they also enjoy devoting a little extra attention to themselves. More unscheduled time is set aside for self interests. Some personal pleasures are pursued without guilt. Little evidence seems to exist that lives of retirees are ruined as a result. Rather, this slight shift in orientation, like that found in the teen years, helps to sense a new beginning taking a deeper root.

Hobbies, personal interests, and long-awaited wish lists are pursued part time or full time. This process depends upon other priorities that are also activated in postretirement. Personal gratification is one of the rewards of retirement and few people detour around this pleasant stretch of the road. The hints below come from experienced travelers:

- Remember some times earlier in life when you felt heavenly. Do the things it takes to recreate that mood, those sensations, and that sweet memory.
- Rediscover serendipity. When an idea floats to the surface, implement it right away. Go to a movie. Buy the sweet smelling bath soap. Read a good book until 4:00 A.M.
- Unleash long-standing interests. Spend the time and money to explore and develop interests to a self-satisfying level.
- Uncover latent abilities. Sign up for some classes, clubs, or activity groups that will draw out your full participation.

- Evaluate the activity calendar for one or two months. Answer the questions: Did I do some things for myself that I really enjoyed? What must I change to make my enjoyment more complete?

QUESTIONS TO PONDER OR DISCUSS:

1. What hobbies, personal interests, and special talents have you enjoyed during your lifetime?
2. Which of them do you anticipate will continue in retirement years? Why?
3. What new skills, knowledge, and personal interests do you hope to pursue in retirement?
4. What aspects of retirement will help or hinder your pursuit of individual desires and intentions?
5. With whom can you openly and honestly share how happy you are and what creates joy in your life?

CHAPTER NINE

Continuing with Educational Options

Severing the cord to the educational community need not be complete or immediate, even in retirement. Retirees have marketable skills, abilities, and experiences honed within educational settings. These qualifications make retirees superb recruits for many school vacancies, and many educators decide to explore those options on a part-time or full-time basis.

ON-CALL SUBSTITUTE TEACHING

School districts seldom have a substitute teacher list that is too long or that is filled with highly experienced and licensed educators. Retirees hold both qualifications and are usually warmly welcomed. The appeal of schedule flexibility remains high for the retiree and a continued association with students and staff members brings pleasure and supplemental income.

Waldo   Prior to retirement, I never thought I would one day return to the classroom, especially the very rooms where I had taught all those years. However, I sorely missed the contact with students. Former colleagues told me they missed me; indeed, I had similar feelings for them, and when an advertisement for substitute teachers caught my eye, I thought, "Why not?" The beauty of substitute teaching is that I am still in control of my own schedule. I can stipulate that I am not available on Mondays and Fridays; my wife and I can go to our cabin before the weekend rush hits the freeways and then return Monday morning, avoiding the Sunday night freeway crunch.

Dorothy   When I work as a reserve teacher, the surprise expression on the face of former colleagues is often followed with the "Why" question and without exception, a gracious "Welcome back!" Substitute teaching fits my needs perfectly. I can use the income because my stay-at-home-mom years reduced the size of my teacher retirement check. I love the contact with children. I am a good reserve teacher who feels well rewarded when the regular teacher returns and compliments me on the positive reaction of students and the completed lesson plans. Finally, there is still flexibility in my schedule because I can say yes or no when called as a substitute or reserve teacher.

COCURRICULAR AND OTHER SPECIAL ASSIGNMENTS

Many classroom teachers carry extra assignments such as coaching, directors of drama, class advisors, and/or chairpersons of a department. When staff members filling these latter roles retire, the administration sometimes has difficulty finding a replacement. In such cases, the retiring educator is urged to continue the extra assignment even though classroom teaching is ending.

Millie   When I decided to retire from classroom teaching, I wondered if it would be possible to continue as science fair coordinator. I would have even more time to encourage students on their projects and still have time for myself. The administration agreed to let me continue . . . until they could find a suitable replacement. Seven years later, I took the initiative to retire from this special assignment because my husband also retired and wanted to live in a warmer climate much of the year.

Mitch   Our school district faced declining student enrollment when I retired. No new teachers were being employed, so fresh blood was not available in the coaching ranks. Few in our very senior staff were willing any longer to put in the extra hours required for coaching. The superintendent asked me to continue as the football coach even though I was retiring from classroom duties. I knew the kids, was committed to the program, and decided this assignment would not interfere with our winter travel plans in the southern part of the country.

LONG-TERM RESERVE TEACHING

Regular classroom teachers are sometimes absent for longer periods of time for various reasons such as recovery from surgery, childbirth, or accomplishing a special project within the central office. Retired teachers who enjoy working with students and who like the added income step into such assignments without missing a beat.

Nicole   I have accepted several long-term substitute assignments. I enjoy working with the same students day after day. The assignments are usually within my comfort zone (my teaching discipline), and responsibilities are confined to the classroom and do not involve other after-school duties.

Often, the number of secondary school students who register for courses in a particular field of discipline exceeds the number of classes that full-time staff members can teach. In such cases, the administration posts a part-time assignment that continues for one quarter, semester, or the entire school year.

Matthew   This is my fourth year of retirement. At minimum, I have taught one section of students for one semester every year and as many as three sections of students for an entire year. My energy levels remain high at the end of my assignments. The part-time work enables me to spend time on personal hobbies and socialize more outside of school. I get to know a smaller number of students very well because I teach them every day, grade their papers, write college recommendations, and feel very much a part of their growth and development.

ADJUNCT TEACHING IN COLLEGE OR UNIVERSITY

Some retirees report opportunities to teach college or university classes, usually as an adjunct teacher. Institutions of higher learning are often eager to make their courses user-friendly by offering them in the same community where students live and work. Employing local educators with proven credentials rather than sending full-time professors to these more distant locations is cost effective, as well.

Harriet   I was first approached to teach an evening college course when I was still teaching psychology classes at our high school. I felt the honor of invitation, but wondered if the demands on my time would be too great and if college-level students would appreciate my style of instruction. These concerns soon disappeared. When I retired from my school district, I decided to embrace college teaching. My day hours are completely free to do as I please, and the college course brings wonderful, new people into my life each semester.

Joseph   A favorite graduate school professor asked me to be a resource person for one session of his school finance classes. He wanted the graduate students who were all prospective business managers to hear from someone in the trenches. Subsequently, he asked me to teach an entire class session when he was going to be gone. In turn, this led to an invitation from the university to teach the entire course during the summer session. I accepted eagerly. This led to many adjunct teaching assignments relative to school finance, negotiations, and other school business-related fields. When

I retired as the school district business manager, I continued my association with the university. I felt my "shelf life" as a business manager would remain current for at least five years, especially if I invited active business managers to come to my classes as resource persons.

OVERSEAS TEACHING

Less typical, but nonetheless viable, is retirement from a school district and acceptance of a teaching assignment overseas, typically teaching English as a second language. Educators making this choice report much satisfaction in teaching children and youth in new cultures, and in making important contributions to world understanding.

Bill   Each year an exchange teacher from China would come to our high school for one year to help teach Chinese language classes, while teachers from our school district would go to China (each for one semester) to help teach English. When I got to know the Chinese teachers who came to our school and heard stories from returning American teachers, I became more and more excited about teaching possibilities overseas. Finally, I took the plunge myself. Living in China in my own apartment, preparing and eating food bought in the marketplace, and traveling to sites I had only read and dreamed about, filled my need for adventure. But what captured my soul was the yearning for English as a second language by the Chinese students. They wanted to learn and revealed a kind of desperation that won my heart.

RETURN TO REGULAR, FULL-TIME TEACHING

What is clearly demonstrated by stories from retirees is that some retire before they are truly ready. Often, there is a cohort of colleagues who have been together for a long time and who get caught up in retirement conversation (a kind of crowd fervor) that prompts group action rather than individual thought. Returning to full-time teaching subsequently becomes a viable choice.

Bradley   I went to work in a medical genetics lab at the university the day after I retired. After six months, I returned to my old suburban high school to fulfill a full-time, long-term substitute position in chemistry for half a year. After that I worked in the city park and recreation program. After some thought, I decided I really thrived on teaching and wanted to return to it. I missed the interaction with the kids, so I applied for a science position in a core city school system where I have been employed as the physics teacher for this past year and plan to return in the fall.

ASSORTED TEACHING OPPORTUNITIES WITHIN COMMUNITY

The opportunities to teach, following retirement, are very extensive. Among the choices are teaching in alternative schools, tutoring individual students, and instructing classes in adult education. While teaching as a professional is confined to fields of discipline where licensure is acquired, many teaching opportunities following retirement draw upon one's knowledge gained through personal interests, exploration, and private study.

Felix   When I was an undergraduate in college, bridge was the card game of choice. I discovered I was pretty good at it, and my wife and I continued to play all during our years as public school teachers. When I retired, the community education director asked me if I was interested in teaching bridge in an adult education class. It didn't take long for me to decide. I now know people all over our community who are playing bridge and are being helped by the instruction they received in my classes.

Maxine   For many years I taught as a sister in Catholic schools. Worried about my retirement income, I accepted a reading teacher position in a public school, but vowed that someday I would return to the Catholic schools to offer what I could to these students. When my goal of enhanced economic security was met, I retired from public school teaching. Near my apartment is a small Catholic school where I now volunteer, teaching students who are having reading difficulties.

TEACHING OPPORTUNITIES WITHIN OTHER ORGANIZATIONS

Teaching skills and knowledge learned in education can provide linkages to fields of work closely related to education. Telling stories, selling ideas, and opening doors to new possibilities are basic in teaching, and retirees can put these marketable skills to use in a variety of settings. Retiring educators have also earned high credibility, based upon years of study and steady work performance, which can be shared in other organizational environments.

Flora   When my retirement became part of daily conversation, some colleagues urged me to run for a seat on the state board of education. They also helped with the campaign. I got the most votes so I won. All my educational experiences in the classroom and school setting were put to good use immediately, but in a policy-making context. For example, I faced audiences of all sizes and had to hold their attention both before and after the election. I had to decide if a proposed policy would impact the classroom positively or adversely. It really helped being in the trenches all those years. Also, I had to listen to and analyze opinions of other board members, a practice that was ingrained in me during faculty meetings, curriculum committees, and in planning for collective bargaining.

Jim Following a student attitude and behavior survey developed by the Search Institute of Minneapolis, I volunteered to serve on a community-wide task force. I soon found myself sharing survey results with local civic groups, church gatherings, and community agencies. About that same time, the Search Institute started a national initiative, one part of which was a speakers' bureau. I signaled my strong interest, and since retirement, have made over 200 presentations around the country to various audiences, using the very skills and drawing upon the very motivations that prompted my career in public education.

TEACHING WITHIN BUSINESS SETTINGS

The words *teacher* or *educator* are used almost exclusively within school settings. The same words, though titled differently, are also adapted widely in private businesses. This is especially true for those performing services to outside clients or carrying out internal activities that engage employees in learning. Titles like consultant or specialist may replace school-related terms, but the essence of the work being done draws upon the same skills and often a similar knowledge base.

Jenna My interest in, and knowledge about, computers and various other programs grew tremendously during my final years as an educator. When I retired, a former student offered me a job in his business where many employees needed computer training. The job title was Computer Support Specialist. The work was part time and paid well. I said yes. For the first time in my life, I am eligible for year-end bonus distributions.

Luis Many years ago, our school district started an employee wellness program. From the onset I was a committee member. Shortly after I retired, I saw a vacancy notice for an employee wellness coordinator in a local manufacturing plant. I applied and was hired for the half-time position. The hours of duty are at my discretion and the work is so similar to what I did in school that I feel right at home.

MY JOURNEY

My decision to work part time as an educational consultant in the first phase of my retirement resulted in an active campaign to remain connected to the education community. One mentor consultant told me, "Go for the pain, identify what is hurting, and provide relief." I sent a flyer to sixty school superintendents identifying typical problem areas in schools and how my experience, training, and skills as a consultant could improve operations. My first clients came from this advertisement.

I also met with the dean of the college of education in a local university who subsequently appointed me senior fellow and lecturer of record, both paying positions. I expressed strong interest in the research done on youth by a nonprofit organization. This resulted in a meeting with the president and a contract to speak about the organization and its research to groups around the United States. Meanwhile, I continued subscriptions to professional magazines, attended professional conferences, and remained updated and conspicuously active to potential clients.

CONCLUSION

The most natural fit between an educator's résumé and possible positions following retirement continues to be in education. Experience and training are concentrated in this field. People in the profession know you and you know them. When you knock, doors open; that doesn't guarantee employment, but it does guarantee an audience and additional opportunities to network. Proceed with the following:

- An updated résumé, professionally portrayed. Present yourself well. Don't assume that past friendships or associations alone will guarantee a position.
- Current recommendations from multiple people, both those who know you as an educator and those who know you in a nonschool setting.
- Readiness to answer interview questions. Anticipate and practice answering them.
- Clarity of thought about your strengths and strong interests. Make a mental note of your deficiencies and what will be said if a question is asked about areas of weakness.

- Preferences regarding work location, assignments, and remuneration.
- Restrictions you have on months, days, and hours of work.
- List of networks such as personal friends, acquaintances, management personnel in the organization where you have worked, well-connected educators, and advocates who know someone and can put in a good word for you.
- Patience and determination to network, network, and network!

QUESTIONS TO PONDER OR DISCUSS:

1. What skills and knowledge do you employ in your current assignment that would carry over into other similar positions in other organizations?
2. What factors would encourage or discourage you from considering further work within an educational setting?
3. What type of work, if any, in an educational setting will best fit your needs and desires?
4. Will pension payments be affected by your returning to work in an educational setting?
5. With whom can you discuss possible postretirement work opportunities in educational settings? In organizations providing education-related services?

CHAPTER TEN

Responding to Private Sector Alternatives

The nonprofit public education sector of the American economy has many parallels to the for-profit private sector. Those who elect to move into the private sector following retirement consistently report areas of overlap as well as unique differences. For example, diverse personalities, work rules, and stated purposes are present in all organizations, public or private. However, methods of remuneration, means of safeguarding trade secrets and know-how, and measures of accountability can be considerably different among organizations.

OBTAIN ADVICE FROM KNOWLEDGEABLE SOURCE

Most educators have limited, personal exposure to private sector employment. Consultation with others who have this experience can help answer pertinent questions. For example: What positions are available in the marketplace? What type of positions are a good match for educator skills, attitudes, and knowledge? And, how does the educator proceed to learn about vacant positions, application procedures, and the best preparation for interviews?

Bruce   Before I retired, I sought advice from President Paul Olson, Blandin Foundation. Each year, his responsibility included distribution of millions of grant dollars annually to schools, hospitals, and communities across the Midwest. His connection to a host of people in both the public and private sector prompted the interview.

He observed that starting a new vocational or professional pursuit during retirement years is very difficult. Most successful persons find opportunities and/or positions that have as many parallels as possible to their former work. Patterns of behavior that work well in one context transfer most easily to parallel situations, and the human effort required to change behavior patterns to match new situations grows more difficult with passage of time.

RECOGNIZE TIME FACTORS IN DECISION MAKING

By the time most educators retire, they have had many life experiences and have learned much from them. They know, for example, that success in challenging and well-rewarded positions requires a significant investment of time to learn the ropes, prove dependability, and demonstrate results. Also, starting a new business requires a major capital investment. Both of these factors are weighed heavily when private sector work is contemplated.

Victoria   Flexibility is what I most value in retirement. The constant press of students coming and going, fixed schedules determined by others, and factors beyond my control were governors during my whole career in education. I am thinking about work in the private sector, but the only positions that appeal to me are those that allow maximum say-so on how I structure my time.

Clark   When I retired, a wonderful new business opportunity was presented to me. However, I would have had to invest my life savings. I sat on the fence for a long time. In the end, I said no. Investing my financial nest egg was too big a hurdle. So many new businesses fail and I would not have time to recover my losses. Also, projected profits would not occur immediately. The delay might be longer than my remaining years in this life.

JOIN OTHERS ALREADY IN ESTABLISHED BUSINESSES

It is not surprising, therefore, to find that educational retirees who elect to move into challenging private sector roles often report a strong linkage with someone already well established in the business or industry. The relationship helps to open doors to opportunities that match the educator's training, skills, and experience.

Keith   Over the years, my life insurance agent also became my good friend. His business flourished and he expanded into financial planning and investments. He reminded me over and over that he could use a "good man" like me as an associate. When I retired, he formalized an offer of employment that I could not refuse.

Beverly   Most of my younger years were spent at home raising four children. When college expenses loomed, I returned to teaching. My husband died young and unexpectedly, so I reached retirement age as a widow, without an income that would sustain my lifestyle. My oldest son, meanwhile, heads a very successful computer software company. He invited me to work with him in a position that draws upon my teaching skills and appeals to my interest in human development. This job opened a whole new career opportunity for me for which I am most grateful.

Paul   An energy-saving company had a contract in our school district. When I announced my retirement as superintendent, the company proposed that I introduce their services to other school superintendents and business managers within the state. My role would be to open doors in school districts to possible energy-saving ideas. A proposal would then be presented by full-time company salespersons. I accepted the offer. The supplemental income I receive from this part-time work is what my wife and I use for travel expenses.

CONTINUE YOUR OWN BUSINESS

Some educators start their own business prior to retirement, often years before. Usually the work is confined to summer months or is very part time during the school year. When retirement comes, the decision to continue the business or enlarge it becomes a reality.

Charles   Early in my teaching career, one summer a shop teacher and I put decks on our respective homes—kind of a do-it-yourself project. Soon thereafter, other people asked us to do the same for them. Before long, we were doing small remodeling jobs for many people. Over time, we gained expertise in construction and practical know-how as employers. As a former principal, my retirement now opened up twelve months a year to the construction business, and, as they say, the rest is history. Although I later sold the business, I still do small remodeling projects for people who live near our summer lake home.

Kimberly   I took our band students on a performance field trip somewhere in the United States or overseas every other year. I encouraged them to take their cameras and to submit their best shots for judging to be conducted by an impartial jury of people interested in photography. My own interest in photography and equipment grew as a result. Soon I, too, was taking pictures, developing them, and putting them on display. When offers to purchase them came, I saw a small business opportunity looming. After retirement, my husband and I began to travel to little town festivals to display and sell photographs. We have great fun meeting new people and more than cover our expenses.

Bob and Julie   Both of us liked biking on the trails through our community and encouraged others to join us. Often they asked us about types of bicycles and which ones to purchase. Before long, a manufacturer asked us to represent their line of bicycles. Our home garage became our sales office and repair shop. We employed students on a part-time basis to do much of the work. When our business prospered, we bought a building downtown.

Carl   I have a good musical ear, took piano lessons as a boy, and participated in the usual recitals and music competitions. The man who tuned the piano in our home later invited me to join him. He said it paid well and was part time, thus fitting easily into the life of a teacher. I took the training, and have tuned pianos during most of my teaching career. As a retiree, I have added another interest, furniture restoration. I now restore old pianos as well as tune them.

Curtis   In the military service, I played the trumpet at special Marine events like the welcoming of dignitaries. My buddies and I sometimes played for dances in the surrounding community. That pattern of weekend gigs continued in my life as a teacher and principal. At retirement, I formed my own band. We play at wedding receptions, openings of new businesses or clubs, and anywhere where people want to hear our kind of music.

PURCHASE OR START A BUSINESS

More rare, but nonetheless an option, is to purchase an established business or start a new business. The entrepreneurial spirit is alive and well in America, and some retired educators are drawn to the challenges of running a business of their own.

Les   Both my wife and I have always loved lake country. Most of our family vacations were spent on water. The year we retired, we rented a houseboat for the first time. We loved the experience and returned from our water adventure to find a For Sale sign on the marina. In due course, we bought it. The summer work is hard, but we have many months in winter to do equipment repairs, travel to warmer climates, and to visit our children.

Susan   A long-time friend calls his business a "milk cow" because the high profits allow him to invest in other businesses. When I approached retirement, he encouraged me to start my own business and promised to help with finances if my idea and plan was a good one. I am now the "Teddy Bear Lady" whose business is delivering Teddy Bears with individualized poems to people who have birthdays, who are celebrating anniversaries, who are retiring, or who are ill.

HOURLY PAY POSITIONS

Another option in the private sector is to obtain hourly pay positions. Typically, they are plentiful in number, likely to be close to one's residence, and normally pay less. They usually require consistent attendance, good communication skills, and a personality to match the job description. Limited hours of work, all quite predictable, combine with the benefits of supplemental income and positive peer associations to bring personal satisfaction. Such positions may be seasonal, such as helping out during a holiday shopping rush or relieving employees on vacation, or may be year round. Regardless, the job works well with other retirement priorities.

Mary Anne   A local realtor office had need for a part-time receptionist, sometimes on Saturday and frequently during the summer. They wanted someone with people skills and someone who knew the community. I lived and taught in this community my whole professional life. They hired me and I enjoy the busy office with people coming and going.

Phillip   During my thirty-five years of teaching, I purchased most of my yard and shop equipment from the local hardware store. We were on a first-name basis. When I retired, the proprietor asked if I could help out. He said that I knew the store inside and out and that many customers would remember me from school days. He was right on both counts. I especially like the job flexibility because other workers and I can figure out how to cover for one another when something special comes up.

Janet   Our community has a large manufacturing plant that offers tours to school groups and tourists. There are regular tours during the summer months and tours by appointment during the school year. I heard about the tour guide vacancy, applied, and was hired. The pay isn't great, but everything else about the job is perfect for me.

Mark   I enjoy sports, perhaps more than the average person. I played football in high school and college. Our city has several professional sport teams who play either in the stadium or sports arena. When I learned that security guards were being hired who could help with crowd control and still see much of the action on the field, ice, or court, I signed up. The fringe benefit of seeing teams play is more important than the pay. It is like substitute teaching. You can say yes or no to any given assignment.

MY JOURNEY

For several years after I retired as school superintendent, I shied away from employment opportunities within the private sector. I knew the money would be as good as, and perhaps better than, the public sector but I could not shake the feeling of betrayal to a lifetime of public service. Perhaps I did not fully trust myself in selling a product or service, thinking that personal gain might intrude upon honesty and forthrightness. Perhaps I was being an elitist or perhaps I was insecure. In any case, I eventually agreed to represent private companies whose services do, indeed, save schools money or help individuals invest their money more wisely. Another key factor was that each company permitted me great time flexibility in carrying out the work.

CONCLUSION

The private sector employs millions of people, far more than the public sector. The U.S. Department of Labor reports 142,878,000 jobs in October 2002 (Bureau of Labor Statistics 2002). Corporations, businesses, and independent operators generate an ever-expanding list of work opportunities. These employers provide gainful employment; encourage innovation and creativity in production, marketing, and service; give dignity, status, and satisfaction to workers; and pay taxes that support our government (including public schools). Retirees looking for full-time or part-time work should explore these opportunities, and many do.

Retired educators are often uniquely prepared by their ability, training, and experience to work in the private sector and employers are eager to employ them. Educators, often with minimal training and supervision, can immediately help most firms or organizations meet project, service, or product objectives. Educators with years of experience also bring maturity of judgment, whether working for others, or starting or purchasing their own businesses. The question for retirees is how best to enter this world. The following suggestions come from retirees who have made the transition:

- Honestly assess, describe, and list your talents, knowledge, and skills.
- Seek out others who know you personally and professionally to learn if they observe more, less, or different things than you have recorded about yourself.

- Prepare your business résumé. Use models already published or borrow résumés from workers in the private sector that can serve as prototypes.
- Be clear how much and how long you want to work. A prospective employee must be able to meet employer's needs as well as his or her own needs.
- Match your résumé to advertised job vacancies listed in daily newspapers and in weekly tabloids found in many neighborhoods.
- Consider purchasing or starting a new business, possibly a franchise. Consult extensively with lawyers, bankers, accountants, and realtors.
- Consider using an executive search firm or job placement service.
- Talk to the people you know who are already on the inside of companies and who might know something or somebody to help you gain employment.
- Join a support group of people, often found in local churches, who are in job transitions.
- Be patient, show determination, and network, network, and network!

QUESTIONS TO PONDER OR DISCUSS:

1. What skills, knowledge, and experience could you bring to the private sector?
2. What types of job opportunities are open to retired educators where you live?
3. With whom could you consult regarding possible positions in the private sector?
4. If you were to seek, or were offered, employment in the private sector, what are important personal considerations in making the decision?
5. What needs in your life might be met by part-time or full-time employment in the private sector?

CHAPTER ELEVEN

Hearing the Call to Civic Service

The caring hearts of educators are especially evident in calls to community service. An entire book, much less this chapter, could be devoted to example after example of selfless giving to children, causes, campaigns, and charities. The deeply felt values that prompt education as a career choice continue to be manifested in how retirement time is used on behalf of others. Indeed, work schedule restrictions are lifted and meetings and cooperative action during daylight hours open new civic service possibilities for retired educators.

PLACES OF WORSHIP

Churches, synagogues, and mosques are worship centers for a majority of Americans, but they also offer programs and activities that require lay leadership and volunteers. While some retirees withdraw from such active engagement, opining that it is time for younger people to step up to the plate, other retirees recognize that sharing time and talents is a lifetime commission.

Ethan Our church and forty other churches turn their Sunday School rooms into apartments for homeless families for one week at a time, four times a year, on a rotating basis. On any given night, up to forty-eight people are housed through the Families Moving Forward program. My wife and I started as volunteers, supplying meals for these families and sleeping at the church as overnight host and hostess. When a homeless family finds a home, their joy is now our joy. When public policy questions arise about the need for low-cost housing, we have a personal, firsthand knowledge of the need and can speak to it. Our voices are older but wiser.

Abraham Our synagogue provides classes for Jewish children to learn Hebrew. I volunteered to be one of the teachers because I have been blessed by knowing Hebrew and because I want the Jewish heritage to be a vital force in the lives of future generations of my people. One of my rewards is being invited to many Bar Mitzvahs where my contributions to Jewish faith development are recognized and honored.

Rachel   Every Wednesday evening during the school year, our place of worship has a midweek program for elementary-age youth. A call went out for adult table leaders during the evening meal. The three duties are to eat, to listen to the children, and to engage them in conversation. I qualified. At my age, many contemporaries are dying. My age group is shrinking. The youth I meet each Wednesday soften my sadness and help me think positively about the future.

Terri   Contrary to common perceptions, places of worship are filled with people who are not perfect and who are hurting. They seek spiritual answers, but also a community where caring is a centerpiece of fellowship. The Stephen Ministry program trains church members how to listen to hurting people and to guide them to professional help when the occasion warrants. As a retired teacher, I have the time, as well as the heart, for this work. Great confidentiality is practiced within the program. Few people in the pews know that through this ministry hundreds of hurting people have been helped through their hardships and loss. The gratitude of the hurting is shared in spoken word, but even more so in restored relationships and healthy lives.

CIVIC ORGANIZATIONS

Many civic organizations like Rotary, Lions, Kiwanis, and Optimist Clubs have mottos that remind members of a life philosophy, or an attitude, that is to pervade every aspect of life, including business and professional work as well as personal activities. For example, "Service above Self" is the Rotary Club motto. Programs and projects then emerge to put slogans into action.

Barry   I became aware that many children from low socioeconomic areas of our city do not have bicycles to ride. I also learned that a local Wal-Mart sells 5,000 bikes a year, some of which are returned due to some mechanical problem. I like to fix things and asked the store manager if these problem bikes might be given to me to repair, rather than have them sent back to the factory at considerable expense. Last year alone, I fixed sixty bicycles in my garage and distributed them through an inner-city school principal to kids of low socioeconomic families. Other club members have contributed money to purchase helmets so kids can ride safely.

Maureen   I joined a local civic club when I retired to meet new people and work with others on community projects. One such project provides a weekend leadership retreat for high school youth. My role is to work with high school counselors to identify promising youth; arrange for permission slips, transportation, and housing; and find adult volunteers for the learning activities. I spend hours and hours on the Internet working out all the details. My reward is seeing students interact with each other and grow in their leadership skills.

Connor   Our club participates in an international student exchange program for high school youth to promote world understanding and peace. I volunteered to be the youth exchange coordinator for our local club because I love working with kids, believe in the program goals, and, in my retired state, have the time to do a good job. This past year two exchange students came to our club, one from Peru and the other from Brazil. They had an excellent experience. Someday I hope to visit them in their home countries.

COMMUNITY ORGANIZATIONS

In every community, there are organizations that actively solicit volunteer help from the community at large. Sometimes the need is carried by word of mouth or is widely advertised by brochures or public announcements in newspapers or television. Once the human eye sees these opportunities, they seem to pop up everywhere like mushrooms on the forest floor.

Randy   I like working with tools and want to spend some of my retirement time using my skills to help others. That is what I'm now doing at a battered women's shelter where I work as an all-around repairman. Some projects are simple like replacing a screen on the entrance door, putting new glass in a cracked window, or painting a bedroom. Other projects are more complex like remodeling a section of the building. Every nail I pound and every brush stroke I apply saves the shelter money and gives me immense satisfaction.

Haley   Within thirty minutes of my home is a large arboretum that is run by our state university. Horticulture is studied there, and visitors are welcome in the display gardens. Thousands of people enjoy the beautiful flowers, walk down the pathways, and take the one-way road through the forested areas. I am one of the scores of people there wearing a volunteer pin. I have worked in the gift and coffee shop in the main building, as well as the entrance gate to collect a small fee from visitors without an annual pass. But what I like best is to take visitors on a guided tour of the gardens. The arboretum provides orientation and training sessions. I have gained a whole new circle of friends who are also volunteers.

Dirk   Soon after I retired, a neighbor told me about the Big Brother/Big Sister program in which an adult like me is assigned a young person who needs a positive male or female role model. That need squared with what I observed as a teacher, so I listened carefully and joined the orientation class for prospective participants. The young man assigned to me is growing up before my eyes. We fish, see ball games, go to movies, or just walk in a park. We talk on the phone and sometimes we just hang out together. My wife and I travel afar to visit our own children and grandchildren, but this lad is nearby and has become like one of my own flesh and blood.

SELF-INITIATIVES

Some retirees take on service projects that show great individual initiative. The idea may relate initially to a hobby or special interest, or it may float to the surface following conversation with others who share a passion. Such projects bring personal satisfaction and can result in changes that will go on for decades.

Lila   I moved to a beat-up lakeside home upstate when I retired. I fixed up the house and then shifted my focus to the eroding shoreline and the tangled web of weeds in the yard. Soon I found other community members who were concerned about similar things. We formed an alliance for action. Our biggest common project has been to restore an open field to its natural state. To buy the land, we sought grants and did fundraising. To obtain zoning approval, we worked with the city council and county board. To learn about prairie grasses, wild flowers, and legumes, we read books and consulted experts. Our dream has become a reality and children and citizens of all ages can now see how the prairie looked when settlers first arrived.

ABUNDANCE OF SERVICE OPPORTUNITIES

Educators are excellent volunteers and do so generously. Many motives are named. Nearly all want to make a positive difference. Also cited frequently are the need for physical activity, a longing to meet and mix with people, and a desire to be a part of the present and future. Civic service opportunities draw retirees like a magnet. (Names are not printed below to ease reading.)

1. I am reading weekly to young children at the local library.
2. The city park and recreation program is where I volunteer.

3. On election days, I am a poll watcher, which is volunteer work in contrast to poll worker.
4. Ticket taking at school sporting events is one of my volunteer activities.
5. A number of us on our block pick up road trash while taking our morning walks.
6. I drive weekly for the meals-on-wheels program for shut-ins.
7. The community services advisory board is where you will find me once a month.
8. Once a year I count loons on lakes as part of a statewide environmental study.
9. Our hospital has many volunteer positions. My favorite is delivering flowers.
10. I love playing the old songs on a piano. Nursing homes beg me to come.
11. My volunteer work on political campaign committees keeps me very busy.
12. The middle school shop teacher uses me as a volunteer to monitor equipment use.
13. Volunteers, including me, help teach art in our elementary school.
14. Each spring and summer, I volunteer as a Little League baseball umpire.
15. Our school nurses need help screening preschool children. I volunteer.

Too much volunteer work by a retiree can become a problem not unlike too much work prior to retirement. Moderation in all things applies even to public service.

John   For every office and volunteer activity that discontinued when I retired, two more seemed ready to take their place. I have always believed that good stewardship is more than meeting a church pledge or making donations to charity; it is also a personal commitment to use time and talent in community service. I was excited about the invitations to public service for they helped replace the loss of my school family but I overdid it. Soon I had to reduce the load because the associated work as community activist fatigued me. I had forgotten that a man in the sixth decade of life runs out of gas faster than one twenty years younger.

MY JOURNEY

I have learned that not every well-intentioned act of service, however big or small, turns out as expected. One late-winter day, I took my car to the local garage and its car wash. Ahead of me in line was a car at the open door to the empty bay with its hot air and steam rolling out and fogging up the car's windows. I could not see who was inside. After waiting impatiently for several minutes I exited my car, walked forward, knocked on the driver's window, which came down just a crack, and said, "You must move forward to activate the mechanism." The person inside said nothing, immediately shut the window, moved the car forward about two yards, and stopped just short of the activating mechanism.

Whereupon I stepped into the car wash and knocked on the window again. At that precise moment, the car jumped forward onto the activating bar on the floor. Water started spraying over everything, including me. I rushed to the entrance door with my head down and eyes protected by a long-billed cap. I did not see the rapidly descending door and ran smack into it. Stunned, I stopped in my tracks. A moment later the door was down and I said to myself, "You are caught inside a car wash." To this day, I don't know who was inside that car and the object of my good will.

CONCLUSION

Most retirees from education are well aware of public service opportunities and benefits. They recall working side by side with lay citizens on curriculum committees, boards of education, referendum initiatives, and homeroom activities. Retirees can recite from their own volunteer experience, because they are usually generous with their time and talents in community life. Retirement for most is not a time to depart from such volunteer activities, but to enlarge the number of them and increase hours of service. The rewards are many:

- Meeting new people and filling the social needs of self and others.
- Learning new skills, knowledge, and attitudes, thus stretching body, mind, and heart.
- Helping to make the present and future brighter for the young, old, or less fortunate.
- Providing expertise that many organizations cannot financially support.
- Feeling the warmth of belonging to community and counting as a valuable member.
- Seeing the linkages among separate groups and organizations, noting how each helps to make the sum total greater than the parts.
- Watching new leadership emerge and develop and giving encouragement to those moving toward the center stage and recognition to those moving on.

- Observing from a front row seat the unfolding of human drama, like a stage play with no ending.
- Having something significant to share with others and helping to keep conversations relevant, refreshed, and rejuvenated.

QUESTIONS TO PONDER OR DISCUSS:

1. Who do you know is actively involved in volunteering? What motivates them?
2. What values come to your mind when you think of volunteer service?
3. What concerns come to mind when you contemplate volunteer possibilities?
4. What volunteer opportunities have come to your attention recently?
5. What types of civic service best match your interests and experience?

CONFRONTING INESCAPABLE CHALLENGES

Life routines are broken by retirement. No longer does the clock regulate a time to rise in the morning or when to go to bed. Long-practiced patterns, such as driving to work, parking, greeting associates, and checking the mailbox, cease. The din of students no longer bombards the ears. Missing are shuffling feet in hallways, banging locker doors, scraping classroom chairs, and the crescendo of young voices amassed in the lunchroom or assembly hall. Their absence may be welcome relief or may leave a hole in self-worth, and even a sense of guilt now that paid employment has ended.

Much of the troubled emotion surrounding retirement springs from unanswered questions that can be traced to core issues in life. Section III addresses these major challenges: economic security (chapter 12), relationships (chapter 13), housing (chapter 14), and health (chapter 15). Acknowledging their awesome presence during retirement years, recognizing a variety of available choices pertaining to each, and finding one's own pathway through the maze can create or restore a sense of well-being and peace of mind.

Nearly all retirees face the above-mentioned major challenges. Most work through them and report satisfaction with results, even though sometimes the decisions they reach seem to be polar opposites. Singular answers rarely resolve complex challenges, so section III will relate a multiplicity of choices, each to be gauged and measured against other related issues. These major challenges are not isolated one from the other. Each stands alone like a color in the rainbow, but is perceived best in relationship to other colors—the composite bringing light and hope to retirement years. To that end, section III is devoted.

CHAPTER TWELVE

Gaining and Maintaining Financial Security

Prior to actual retirement, educators name finances as their number one challenge. These same educators report, often with relief, that concerns about financial matters did not materialize once they moved into retirement. This ultimate peace of mind is good news.

Amy   Having sufficient retirement income was my main concern prior to retirement. I didn't really have a good handle on what the teacher retirement system would pay me each month. Since I had a very loose month-to-month budget, I was anxious about predicting expenses years down the road. I did seek and receive answers to my questions. Thankfully, none of my concerns about finances have materialized. I should have gotten help with them much earlier and enjoyed more peace of mind.

CONCERN FOR ECONOMIC SECURITY

Many people who express discomfort with high risk and rapid change enter education. There is a great deal of predictability in the profession. Educators with seniority are seldom laid off. Paychecks are rarely missed. Academic courses may change but always within a field of licensure. Only occasionally must a teacher move to a new location as a result of changes in building assignment. Associates turn over gradually, so social relationships last long and can go deep. In education, stability and security are like sisters. However, the annual salary is usually less than in most other professions.

Ross   A mentor early in my career told me three things: I would never be rich but I would have enough money. My wealth would be found in relationships with people, not products. My legacy would be found in lives of future generations, not fleeting fame, an immobile monument, or a huge estate. I think he was right on all three counts but I needed some reassurance on the first one.

Paul   I was a Depression baby. Over the years of my youth, the anxieties of my father and mother about not having "enough" were passed, in part to me, the oldest of four children. When my wife and I started our careers, we deliberately set money aside for retirement, and when in the last two decades our financial planner said, "Save, save, save," we did so, but not to the exclusion of life's necessities and reasonable perks.

At retirement (and prior to the 2000 market turndown), our financial planner did a 180-degree turn. He urged us to spend investment earnings. He said, "Eat your eggs, but not your chickens." He suggested, for example, that we travel more while health was good. This turnabout in advice made me feel uneasy and somewhat guilty.

By retirement age, most educators are well aware that their level of income is adequate or satisfactory but not excessive, and that the nest egg for retirement is relatively modest. Add the unknown factor of financial needs in retirement, and many educators approach retirement feeling uneasy about finances, and sometimes very insecure.

Alexis   Before my father died, he urged me to get good financial advice and not wait until I retired. He said too many people wait, worry needlessly, and do not monitor their progress on a financial plan that will meet retirement needs. I took his advice and have never regretted it. I carefully selected my doctor, dentist, banker, lawyer, clergy, and now include the financial planner, too.

Brian   I began saving money early in my career. Not much, mind you, but something from every check through payroll savings. At first, I left the money in regular savings accounts, and then moved it to certificates of deposit that yielded a little more interest. From there, I moved into the purchase of some stocks and bonds based upon what I'd heard from friends and read in popular magazines. The market moved up and down, and I was proud to tell others of my successes and reluctant (embarrassed) to share losses. Too many choices and decisions seemed off cycle; that is, because I bought too high and sold too low, my doubts as an independent investor grew.

TURNING TO A FINANCIAL PLANNER

Trusting another person to advise you regarding investment of life savings is a huge decision. The title "financial planner" is widely used, but there are clear distinctions among these service providers. One of the first questions to ask is with whom the financial planner is affiliated.

Wayne   The financial planner I selected is affiliated with a large financial services firm (formerly called a brokerage house). The research department keeps him informed about marketplace conditions and what the experts determine are good stocks, bonds, and other financial securities to buy and sell. In turn, he makes his recommendations to me and helps me understand how decisions will affect my overall financial plan.

Samantha   Early in my career, I purchased a life insurance policy. Subsequently, my insurance agent explained that his company also provides a number of investment opportunities in addition to insurance. Because he already knew my situation, I listened to his advice. In effect, he has become my financial planner.

Austin   My decision has been to go with an independent financial planner. She is knowledgeable in the investment field and has access to a wider variety of financial instruments than any single brokerage house or insurance company can offer. I like the feeling that she is working only for me, not some parent company.

Another question that should be asked is how the financial planner will be paid, inasmuch as the means of payment varies.

Martin   Like the traditional stockbroker, my financial planner receives his income from a surcharge that accompanies every purchase or sale he handles. When transactions in my account are more frequent, more charges are generated. Churning is the term used to describe unwarranted buy/sell orders. When my mother-in-law died, I became the administrator of her estate and saw a record of transactions that was far in excess of what constituted good judgment in my mind. My advice is to monitor your portfolio carefully when per transaction fees are charged.

Jessica   Quite frankly, I don't know how much my financial planner is paid. He is associated with an insurance company who pays him directly when I buy an insurance policy or any other financial product sold through the company. I recognize two dangers: (1) the products made available to me may be what the company has to offer rather than what I really need, and (2) the payment to the agent may be excessive but that is hidden from me. It comes down to my trust in the company and the insurance agent.

Natalie   Annual payments to my financial planner are related to my total assets. I pay a fee based upon a percent of total assets invested. That percent figure can vary from one planner to the next or be on a sliding scale depending upon the size of portfolio. Remuneration for services rendered is tied partially to portfolio performance. When overall assets grow, both the investor and planner benefit. The converse is also true. One risk is that a financial planner can become more interested in new clients rather than serving old ones. Inactivity in a portfolio still results in charges. My advice is to select a financial planner carefully and note how well your portfolio is administered.

Ned   Over the years, I have used financial planners from large financial institutions, insurance companies, and independent companies. There are advantages and disadvantages to each. Larger companies seem to have more checks and balances but seem more constrained in responding to my unique needs. Independent financial planners have to do more of their own research in a very large marketplace and tend to work out of smaller offices. I consult with colleagues and friends regarding their experiences, but in the end I usually trust my own instincts in selecting and working with a financial planner.

INTROSPECTION, A CRITICAL COMPONENT

Thorough financial planning begins with questions like these: What is current income? What are current expenses? What savings have been accumulated? What are outstanding debts? What are projections in each category at the point of retirement? Will current trends achieve retirement goals? How much tolerance is there for investment risk? The answer to the latter question can encompass serious nail-biters who worry over every dollar to carefree gamblers who are excited by chance.

Jane   I am an abstract, random type of person and my financial affairs showed it when my financial planner and I first met. We hit it off very well, although her questions forced me to look at my life in a structured way that was foreign to me. For the first time, I saw on paper where I was spending my money. As a result, I developed estimates of future teacher retirement checks, Social Security payments, and likely income from investments. Together, they did not yield the income needed to meet my retirement goals, which included much travel and some expensive hobbies. We developed a plan that is working for me. The financial planner helped me see the big picture and encouraged me to stick to the game plan. That accountability was critical in my case.

ASCERTAIN INCOME STREAM

Most city or state retirement programs provide estimates of retirement income related to years of projected service and earned income. Also, most retirement programs offer multiple options regarding payout.

Melissa   Twelve months before my retirement, I met with financial counselors associated with the state's retirement program for educators. It was a wise move. First, I learned that one additional year of teaching would maximize my retirement payments. Deciding to teach just one more year became a no-brainer. Second, I learned about the accelerated payment option. That is, I could choose (or decide against) accelerated payments for a few years, followed by smaller payments thereafter. The option would provide more state retirement money before Social Security paychecks begin to arrive, and less thereafter, thereby providing a more even flow in retirement income. The counselor helped me understand all available options.

Jonathan   I am losing $10,000 per year in retirement pay because I was too stubborn or too busy, or both, to meet with the state retirement officials and learn about all the possibilities for increasing retirement benefits. A new state law had been passed that I didn't know about, that allowed a school district to authorize a leave of absence for up to five years for career exploration elsewhere. I could get retirement credit for each of those years if the associated payments into the retirement system continued unabated either by employee full pay, employer full pay, or by combination pay. I missed the train on that one. Be sure to tell others my story but not my name.

Not all state or city retirement plans, of course, include the Social Security option, and Social Security itself includes options. Understanding the Social Security contribution to the income stream is a must.

Amanda   I never gave much thought to Social Security. The deduction was automatically removed from each paycheck. A Social Security notice in the mail came saying I could request a copy of my record and it is a good thing I did. Somehow a glitch occurred in years of credit under my maiden name and married name. It was straightened out in due course and they sent me an estimate of my retirement benefits under different age scenarios. All this information helped me figure out an optimum plan for drawing income from both teacher pension and Social Security.

Caleb   My wife and I thought our total income would be quite sufficient at our retirement, but we were concerned about what would happen if I died first. I knew my teacher retirement payment would continue to go to her but would be cut 50 percent. Would that also happen to Social Security? Clearly, her living expenses would not be reduced 50 percent if she remains in the same house and operates the same vehicle. We made an appointment with the Social Security counselor and got the answers we needed.

Dean   My twin brother and I teach in different states so we compare similarities and differences in all aspects of our careers. My state retirement plan is coordinated with Social Security, so my retirement income will come from both sources. His state retirement plan isn't so coordinated, thus he will not receive a Social Security payment unless he works in a nonschool setting to earn enough work-units to quality for Social Security.

Educators with long service are often eligible for a severance package. Several choices face the retiree if this end-of-career boon becomes reality.

Ashley   As our faculty became older, more interest was shown in master agreement language pertaining to severance. Different factors figure into the mix, including years in the district, unused sick leave days, and salary level the last year of work. I had not calculated the numbers for myself until I retired, but I was very pleasantly surprised by the amount.

Connor   I had several options relating to my severance at the point of retirement. One was to take it in lump sum or spread it over a multiple-year period. My income-tax man helped me with this question. Then the expenditure options had to be addressed: make a one-time larger purchase, add severance to the investment portfolio, or spend it gradually like pocket money.

Last, and hopefully not least, most retirees can turn to private investments in retirement. Once again, multiple options present themselves.

Doris   Early in financial planning for retirement, my financial planner posed two very different scenarios. One was to leave a financial legacy to others, for example, my children, a favorite charity, or a foundation dedicated to a cause of my choice. The second was to estimate my time of death and spend all of my investment assets by that projected date. The second option was right for me for many reasons. My challenge was to identify a date when I would likely die so that the monthly payout could be determined accordingly. I reviewed the health history of my parents and grandparents as well as my own. None of them lived past the age of eighty-five, so I selected that date and added five years for good measure (age ninety).

Ryan   My mother died first, then my father. My three siblings and I were surprised by the size of our inheritance because Dad was not lavish in his spending and was very secretive about his financial affairs. Good stewardship was such a big part of his life. My retirement plan is to use half of each year's investment income to supplement my other income and reinvest the other half so that my portfolio will more than keep up with inflation. I'd like my children to be surprised like I was by the size of the inheritance and be reminded one last time of our family's value system.

Jenna   My retirement income is almost the same as it was when I was teaching. I don't need additional income from investments. My plan is not to touch it and let it grow as market conditions permit. Half will go to my nephews and niece. The other half will go to my church.

The investment strategy used for portfolio assets plays a big role in its value as well as derived income for possible use in retirement. This cold, hard fact gives rise to a maze of alternatives that sound right to one investor and not the next.

Isaiah   When my parents died, I inherited the house and decided to rent it out rather than sell. The house appreciated in value, as did the rent. This led me to put more and more of my retirement nest egg into real estate. If I can't handle the work directly, I employ a real estate management company. Sure, there are headaches and some risks with this strategy, but all other investment options have their downsides, too.

Stephanie   Taking big chances is not my make-up. Neither do I like to spend much time on money matters. My strategy is to purchase U.S. savings bonds or treasury bills and certificates of deposit. I believe in the ladder-approach in which a given amount of money is invested on a regular basis, regardless of marketplace conditions. Over time, the returns vary from high to low but the principle remains intact and can be reinvested at renewal times.

Gretchen   Years ago, my financial planner recommended an investment strategy that I have followed to this very day. He explained to me that younger investors have regular (and growing) income to pay their bills and typically do not count on investment income for current bills. A market downturn or risky investments that falter do not prompt an immediate (bill-paying) crisis. Not so for retirees who count on investment returns to help meet current expenses. Following this advice during my working years, I gradually decreased the proportion of my assets from equity investments and increased the proportion in fixed-income type of investments.

Ted   Thank goodness, I diversified my portfolio. I put nearly all of my investments into well-managed, diversified mutual funds rather than investing them heavily in one sector of society like technology or one company like Enron, which suffered a total collapse. In the 1990s, my portfolio did not grow as rapidly as reported by some other colleagues who invested in dot-com companies, but neither did my portfolio suffer severe losses when the economy went into recession after 2000, and again when the marketplace took a severe downturn after September 11, 2001. My retirement nest egg has taken hits but has not tanked. Many of my colleagues have not fared as well.

RECOGNIZE AND MANAGE BUDGET EXPENDITURES

A budget before and after retirement obviously has two sides: income and expenditures. Many educators assume retirement expenditures are less, but their reported experiences say "maybe yes" and "maybe no." The expenditure side of the budget equation also requires diligence.

Forrest   When my wife and I projected our retirement expenditures, what first came to our minds was the end of mortgage payments, less need for new clothing, paid off college loans for our children's education, and a reduction in monthly automobile payments. We assumed our need for newer, more dependable automobiles to get to and from work would no longer have high priority.

In fact, our mortgage payments have ended, but we know now that property taxes and insurance costs that had been bundled within the monthly mortgage payment do not end; indeed, they continue to rise. Sure, we wear well-used clothes around the house and in the yard, but when we go out, we want to look reasonably prosperous so the amount we spend for clothing has changed little. What did change is the type of clothing we now purchase. We continue to drive two cars; we like the independence of coming and going. Furthermore, we do not like the idea of being stranded along some roadside, especially at our age, so we continue to drive automobiles that are less than four years old. Overall, our predicted expense reductions in retirement have not materialized.

Virginia   I have been our family's bookkeeper our entire married life. In retirement, we have experienced a higher level of spending, not less. Each of us has more time to pursue our hobbies, such as golf for which there are fees, and enjoy professional performances, like the theater, orchestra, athletics, and so forth, for which there are expensive tickets. We have been able to travel twelve months of the year, not just summer and during other school holidays, so those budget expenses have increased significantly. We entertain more; our food budget reflects this expanded hospitality. Thankfully, the income side of our retirement budget is able to cover these additional, and somewhat underestimated, expenses.

Many retirement dreams include extended winter vacations in warm climates and the appeal of one's own summer place in the mountains, along a seacoast, or at the lake. Entirely new categories are thereby added to the budget.

Landis   Our retirement dream was to sell our home and move to the mountains where we had enjoyed so many summer vacations. Little did we anticipate the powerful draw of grandchildren who live near our family home. At our retirement, our hearts were torn between little ones hugging us (and we them) and our long-time dream of a mountain home. Our solution was to sell our long-held family home, rent an apartment nearby, and purchase property in the mountains. Now we have not only payments associated with two residences, but also the cost of transportation back and forth many times a year.

Additional expenses in retirement arise even though one elects to stay in the same residence. What comes to mind either gradually or like a sharp jolt is that furniture bought twenty-five or more years ago has become badly worn or is out-of-date. Likewise, kitchens and bathrooms reflect their age, and maintenance and replacement of outdoor landscaping is an ongoing obligation with home ownership.

Bert   My dad lived until he was in his late eighties in the family home. Mom died much earlier. When we visited him, the house felt warm and comfortable to my brother, two sisters, and me because it brought to mind childhood memories. Following his funeral, we all returned to the house for coffee and decision making about the estate. Our eyes suddenly looked at the house as a prospective buyer. We saw old paint colors, worn carpets, scratches on cabinets, outdated bathrooms, and overgrown bushes and trees in the yard. Only the kitchen had a phone, and it was the old dial type.

Hattie   My husband and I decided that we wanted to remain in our family home as his dad had done. An alternate choice was to move into a shiny, new condominium with up-to-date furniture, bathrooms, kitchens, color schemes, and all the modern conveniences, as was being done by many friends about our age. Our decision was "fight" rather than "flight." Over the last ten retirement years, we have installed new windows, siding, and kitchen cabinets. New furniture graces our bedroom, living room, and dining area. Last year, a contractor put in new shrubs and flowers to bring our landscaping up to par with the neighborhood. Next on our list are the bathrooms. Our family home may not be in the Parade of Homes, but it remains up to date.

Even more routine budget items must be pondered carefully in making expense projections. Recognizing inflation and other factors impacting costs of products, services, and taxes improves the validity of estimates.

Eric   Our home is rapidly rising in market value, and the tax rate that is also climbing is applied against that growing valuation. The combination scares us. Furthermore, our house insurance coverage must keep up. The premiums are going sky high. Will we be able to afford this home throughout our retirement?

Emma   Heck to the often-cited annual cost of living index! It may apply to prices for groceries and clothing, but what about utility costs? The budget categories most difficult for us to predict are health insurance and drug costs. They seem to be on an endless, double-digit course.

Anthony   Our expenses have risen in retirement but so have payments from the state retirement program and Social Security. We managed our expenditure budget carefully during our working years and the same good stewardship works in retirement. I haven't heard too many retirees from my profession say they don't have enough to live on.

PREPARE FOR ESTATE TRANSFER

Pension payments end at life's end, but owned property, life insurance, and investment assets constitute the estate that goes to others by plan or default. Financial planning is not complete unless it includes the estate as a whole. Thorough and timely estate planning is good stewardship and is one last gift that is given to the people left behind.

Colley   Our estate is much larger than I could ever have realized on a teacher's salary, thanks to my wife's inheritance. Our financial planner and attorney helped us work through many estate issues. This is just a partial list. How would estate matters be handled when one or the other of us died? Did we need or want a trust? Should our children be involved in its administration? Who else, if not one of our children? Do we want to lower tax consequences on the estate? Are there institutions and charities to which we want all or a portion of the estate to go? Do we wish to donate gifts to such people or causes while we are yet living? By the time we were done, we had reflected on our values, relationships, and convictions, made a living will, revised our last will and testament, and made some difficult choices.

Jennifer   Our financial planner made two recommendations about our estate. First, we should organize our estate records carefully. So we did. We made a list of all our assets, where the associated paperwork could be found (our home safe, safety deposit box at the bank, file drawer, etc.) and its estimated value. We told our children, attorney, accountant, financial planner, and estate administrator where the list was kept. Every year, after New Year's Day, we update it.

Second, we should simplify our estate. Maybe we have gone overboard, but I don't think so. We consolidated CDs into larger amounts and keep them in fewer institutions. We had a garage sale, have given away things we no longer need, and have identified who in our family should receive special heirlooms like family photos, furniture made by grandpa, and quilts made by grandma.

Jack   With advancing age, my wife and I have simplified our estate many different times. Following my mother's death, my siblings and I felt free to sell the family farm. When our energy level could no longer take care of our large family home and cabin, we moved into a very nice, but smaller, townhouse. When arthritis got so bad in my joints, we sold the lake place lock, stock, and barrel. When my wife's heart problem grew worse, we sold our townhouse and moved to our current address, a retirement center with three types of living quarters: independent living, assisted living, and nursing care. Each transition has left us with fewer material possessions, but we made the decisions while we yet could. Thankfully, we still have each other and our loved ones. That is what really counts.

Many educators grapple with what heirs are told about estate contents prior to the time of death. Should offspring be left guessing about their parents' estate or be informed in part or in detail while the parents are still living? Reports from retirees provide a wide range of options with no alternative holding favor over others.

Max   My dad asked me, his oldest child of four, to be his estate administrator and openly shared his financial affairs with me when he turned sixty-five, a year after my mother's death. He requested that I not reveal this information to the other siblings, and he himself told them that I would be his confidant and hold the power of attorney. Every year, Dad and I met to update his net worth, review his records, and go over his wishes regarding his living will, funeral homes, church service, and burial place. Three years ago, he died. I had no problems with probate, and there is yet an abundance of good will among all family members.

Marjorie   I loved my parents. I was their only child. They were so good to me during my growing years and expressed pride in my choice of teaching as a career. I promised in my heart to take care of them to the best of my knowledge during their retirement years. They turned aside my delicate inquiries into their financial affairs. Then, at the age of seventy, a terrible car accident took both their lives in the blink of an eye. I was devastated and learned subsequently from their attorney that I was to receive the entire inheritance. It was a considerable sum, sufficient to cover both of them had they required nursing home care for years and years. How I wished that they had been more open with me. Even a hint would have freed me from much unnecessary worry.

Marty   Dad had a tremendous head for business, and his drive to succeed financially resulted in rare hours at home with me and my two brothers. None of us worried about money. Dad reassured us he would leave us well off. My older brother followed in Dad's footsteps and succeeded in the business world. I followed in my mother's footsteps, becoming a teacher after some years of travel. My younger brother never took hold of his life; indeed, alcohol and drugs became a mainstay in spite of multiple rehabilitation clinics. I think Dad's promise of a large inheritance played a role in wrecking his life.

MY JOURNEY

Regarding fiscal management, I recall scores of references to money in the Bible, none saying that wealth is bad—but all warn that the passion to possess things can destroy a righteous life. The last of the Ten Commandments, for example, reminds me "not to covet." I find myself fighting strong impulses to have and to hold; I try to smother them with more altruistic thoughts and action.

CONCLUSION

Nearly all retirees who shared concerns about finances prior to their retirement report that postretirement financial problems did not become reality. The decision-making processes that worked well during the working years served their purposes also during retirement. There are exceptional cases, however, that help reinforce the guidelines cited below:

- Utilize the services of a good financial planner.
- Know your own values, what you hold most dear, and how they relate to financial planning.
- Invest throughout a career, following a wise strategy that recognizes present tolerance for risk as well as the financial targets necessary to realize future dreams.
- Predict and plan for both income and expenditures in retirement, including a realistic appraisal of living costs and the temptations to overspend.
- Formalize estate records and associated distribution plans.
- Finally, decide who is designated to carry out estate plans, and what is shared with others about the estate prior to death.

QUESTIONS TO PONDER OR DISCUSS:

1. Who is your financial planner and what are his or her qualifications for this critical role?
2. How thoroughly have you identified your life values and correlated current and future income and expenses?
3. What investment strategies are you employing and how well do they mesh with your personality, tolerance for risk, and future retirement goals?
4. What is your net worth and what are the major assets within your estate? What preparations have been made to transfer the estate to others?
5. Whom have you designated to handle your affairs in case of illness or death, and what do you think should be told to others about your estate ahead of that time?

CHAPTER THIRTEEN

Maintaining and Replacing Relationships

Individuals who are drawn into the field of education and remain for a full career typically care about people. They enjoy the intellectual stimulation and social dimensions of daily contacts with students, their parents, and work associates. Some relationships are very close. Some associations are casual. Educators find themselves with a myriad of relationships that create community and a deep sense of belonging that is dramatically changed by retirement.

Ruth Ann   During my whole career, I looked forward to school. Everyday, my fellow teachers and I would arrive about the same time, pick up our mail near the principal's office, go to the preparation desks in the department office, and then head to first-hour classrooms. Some of us had joint preparation periods and ate lunch together. After school, we served on some of the same committees and always attended faculty meetings, sitting together as a department. We respected and genuinely liked one another. Retirement posed a great loss for me in companionship and collegiality.

Jason   Not until retirement plans were well on their way did I realize how much of my life revolved around school. Most of my friends are teachers and administrators. Most of my entertainment occurs at sport events, school plays, and choir concerts. Educators fill graduate classes. Colleagues and I are together in local workshops. Even my after-school hours are filled with thoughts about students, staff, lesson plans, and school events. Outwardly, I said that I could handle this retirement business, but inwardly I already missed these companions in life and wondered who and what would or could fill the void.

AWKWARD TIMES

Professional workers in education depend upon one another for task completion and social interaction. Long-term coworkers are predictable. Associates know what and what not to expect in most situations. There is comfort in this knowledge. Positive relationships grow. Routines become established. Everyone's performance moves higher on the productive scale. Retirement interrupts this forward progress and can create new dynamics and awkward times.

Tad   For twenty-eight years, I was one of six elementary principals and was the most senior administrator in the whole district at the time of my retirement. Superintendents would come and go; each new one would consult me to learn about "history" in the district. In many respects, I served as principal-at-large, as well as elementary principal. What caught me by surprise was my sense of powerlessness in the last year of work. Consultations ended. New committees were started without me. Negotiations excluded me. My title had not changed, but my involvement level and the associated ego boosts were subject to a bruising.

Leif   People involved in hiring my replacement stopped their conversation or gracefully shifted it when I entered the room. Of course, I did not want to butt into their business, and they did not want to hurt me in any way as my days to retirement wound down. An unwritten understanding developed. Coworkers would not include me in their replacement planning; I would not ask about progress, and together we would stay in the safety zone.

REACHING OUT

Some retirees report a conscious preretirement effort to intensify social relationships, particularly with school friends. The intent is to strengthen the friendships and possibly elongate them into retirement itself.

Jeanine   Prior to my retirement, school was "my family," was most of my entertainment, and was the touchstone to friendships. When I decided to retire, I felt a kind of desperation. Most of my school friends were younger and not retiring. I would no longer see them every day. I found myself asking them to do things with me after school and on weekends that far exceeded our past associations. I sought reassurances that they would not forget me.

A smaller percentage of retirees report an opposite reaction. For them, seeing and being with friends and associates is a painful reminder of the coming separation. They pull away from school social interactions, attempting thereby to lower the level of anxiety. Coping includes a conscious reduction in the frequency and depth of school social relationships.

Grace   My initial reaction was to pull away from these dear people. I wasn't sleeping well, got up earlier, and arrived in school before the others. I did more preparation in my own classroom and found someplace to eat by myself. Once during inclement weather, I ate my lunch in my car and was found out. My department chairperson invited me in for a chat, not to scold or chastise, but to note the change in my lifetime patterns and express the concerns of departmental members. I began to see that my hurting self was hiding from the very people who wanted to support and love me. My self-absorption was immature and dysfunctional.

Others report an outward marshaling of effort, away from the school setting, to make new friendships and rekindle old ones. Filling the anticipated gap in interpersonal relationships may be a conscious, high-energy effort or just a slight shift in focus to surrounding people.

Eric   No one in school who knew me would accuse me of being a social animal. Staff members respected me and I them, but our relationship was professional, not deeply personal. My sense of community and belonging at the time of retirement was not dependent upon school associations. I knew that interpersonal relationships I lost at school would be made up by spending more time at church, with neighbors, or with my immediate and extended family.

SAYING GOOD-BYE

Rituals are as important in retirement as they are in other aspects of life. They bring people together who share a common bond. They allow and, indeed, encourage expression of thoughts and feelings that otherwise remain unspoken. Rituals provide processes that bring together past memories in life and future hopes and dreams in a special alchemy that help people through a transitional time.

Megan   When I announced my retirement, one teacher after another came to my room to wish me well and acknowledged our special friendships over the years. Sometimes the conversation was brief, ending with the words "Good luck," and other visits were longer and included trips down memory lane. I was grateful they came to me one at a time rather than as a group. I wasn't yet ready for what was to come later.

Howard   Every year, the administration designates one spring day as Employee Recognition Day. Among the festivities, retirees are publicly honored with a red rose to wear for the day plus an afternoon ceremony where each retiree is given a good-bye gift, usually a desk set with a clock. For a long time, I minimized the importance of this ceremony but when my turn came, I thought and felt differently. We all need a forum to affirm what we have given to each other over the years, to express our feelings, and to acknowledge formally that we counted in the trenches of life. Moreover, we find courage to acknowledge that we will all somehow survive what comes next.

Nora   My retirement party tested me and left me exhausted. The top administration changed in our district and with it a positive work environment. Many administrators left or retired like me. I felt sadness, anger, and resentment that I was leaving after thirty-five years with a bad taste in my mouth. I reflected grace and good humor even though I was extremely sad at the time. It was hard work. I did not want to influence other colleagues negatively with my decision, nor did I want to damage the reputation of others by acting out the part of one of the rats leaving the sinking ship. I tried to be positive about my retirement to others so that I would not have regrets about being disloyal.

Kevin   My last day will be remembered forever. Students left the previous day. I came to work expecting it to be a clean-up and clear-out day. Instead it was one long celebration. It was like a broken dike with pent-up emotions bursting forth: a big cake, thank-you speeches, and future well-wishing. Story after story flowed from times past, some true and others far from anything I recognized. I wish everyone this same career cap of affirmation, thanksgiving, and gratitude.

SELF-IMAGE ADJUSTMENTS

Vocation is among the first things named when people are asked to describe themselves. What we do is so highly valued that other descriptors of self are named later, if at all. I am a teacher. I am a principal. I am superintendent. I am an educator. These words flow early and often during working years. As a career unfolds, it is increasingly difficult to think of one's self apart from professional activities and the work place. Retirement from work poses a radical departure for many educators in how self is defined.

Cameron   Going through retirement ceremonies clarified for me that I was leaving a clearly defined role, respected by the world, and rewarded by social acceptance, pay, and applause. These questions began to preoccupy my thinking: Who am I becoming? What will be my new "I am"? What purposeful role is mine after retirement? How does a retiree maintain or gain a measure of self-worth? I answered these questions in due time, but certainly not right away.

Bette   I never thought as a school counselor that one day I would be the one being counseled. Little did I realize how much I depended upon the students with problems, parents with concerns, administrators with paperwork, and teachers with complaints about this or that pupil. I was a "fixer" or at least I tried to be. Year after year, this went on until I finally retired. Then I discovered the work and self-sacrifice of all those years was really my underpinning of self-worth. My apartment seemed empty and smaller. Time hung heavy. I moped around. I was at a loss to put together a new life that had the same degree of meaning and purpose as the one I left. I was in a tailspin. Thankfully, I found a counselor to help me through a very rugged phase of my retirement.

Savannah   My self-esteem came back full steam when I began to realize that I am many things besides an educator. I am a wife, mother, grandmother, sister, aunt, musician, neighbor, community volunteer, church officer, charity donor, and friend. I am thoughtful, honest, responsible, caring, generous, and dependable. Retirement may have ended my love and service in the school setting but not in every other sphere of my life. Once this orientation shift was complete, I felt whole again.

FAMILY TRANSITIONS

Educators are practiced in verbal communication. Retirement changes many of the parties who talk to one another and also many of the subjects discussed, but the habit of talking to other people continues. People living together in retirement listen to each other many more hours each day. School-related topics of conversation that once filled evening hours mostly end. New topics fill both day and evening hours.

Nina   My husband and I retired six months apart. Our common interests remained the same, grown children, house management, and college friends, but we had so many more hours to fill as a married couple. He wasn't that interested in education, nor was I in engineering, and neither of us was fully engaged on the professional front any longer. We love each other and like time together, but there are limits to every good thing. We determined in retirement to spend additional time away from each other in personal pursuits that matched our separate interests and also vowed to find more common interests. He's now into computer classes held at the city hall for seniors, and I'm in a book club and Bible study. Together, we attend the civic concert series and play cards with some new neighbors. We got through an awkward time in our married life and are enjoying our retirement.

Much privacy is lost when couples retire. The hours that are spent together nearly doubles.

Marcy   Our first inclination as a retired couple was to do everything together that once had been done separately. We found ourselves in the same car and same places for hours on end: shopping for groceries, visiting nearby grandchildren, going to the library, voting at elections, going to movies, and watching TV. The other person is always present and accountability for time and action increases, too. Little irritants started growing into big ones. We each needed our own spaces and began to work out compromises that would help both of us enjoy retired life.

Walter   I was a school principal. My wife, a nurse, retired one year before me. What a surprise she had for me when, after a couple of months into my retirement, she said, "Walter, we have to have a serious talk. You are driving me nuts!" She then unloaded.

I was spending too much time in the kitchen. I had sorted through and rearranged all the drawers and storage spaces. Cooking for her was now much more difficult. I put the recipe books into alphabetical order rather than their usual most-to-least used order. Cupboards were overfilled with canned goods I had purchased and placed on top of one another so they often fell when she reached up high for them. The most recent thing was that I cleaned the kitchen stove from one end to the other the day before the cleaning lady was to come. Apparently, I also was beginning to make strong suggestions on what we should be eating.

Honest, I was just trying to be helpful. I saw ways to save time and make things work more efficiently. I had time on my hands and was taking on domestic projects in lieu of school ones. She charged me to back off, go back to work (someplace, anyplace, and soon) or find some meaningful time-fillers away from the house.

Frustrations build when anticipated pleasures in retirement years give way to inescapable family responsibilities. Regret and anger fall as heavily upon the retired as any other age group, and perhaps more so because less time remains for resolution. Family issues contribute a significant share of relationship challenges in retirement.

Pat   When my husband's mother died, his father moved into our home for what we thought would be a short period of time. That was three years ago, shortly after we retired. He is elderly and doesn't drive any longer. In fact, he can't be left alone except for short periods. His arrival and stay has put a severe cramp on our retirement plans.

Daniel   Retirement from a superintendent position in Wisconsin allowed us to sell our family home and move to Arizona, a move we long anticipated. We had spent much of our vacation time there earlier. Within the first year, our first grandchild was born back in Wisconsin. Numbers two and three came shortly thereafter. We made frequent trips back and forth until the pull of the next generation was too strong. Reluctantly, we sold our Arizona home and returned to Wisconsin.

Maxine   What we thought would be the perfect marriage ended in divorce with our daughter being solely responsible for three children and most of her living expenses. Childcare is so expensive and no suitors are close at hand. My husband and I bought property on a beautiful but distant lake years ago with the intention of developing it during our retirement years. Those plans are delayed because we are the daycare grandparents for two grandchildren. The third is already in elementary school.

TRANSITIONS IN FRIENDSHIPS

Friendships constantly evolve. This lifelong cycle repeats itself over and over—reach out, find, touch, hold, enjoy, and say good-bye. People need one another. This truism also holds for retirees.

Joanne   Once I entered into retirement, most of my strong school connections did not deepen or disappear; rather, they slipped into the category of less frequent. There were more casual contacts into which reminiscences formed the center of conversations. Happily and surprisingly, when many of these good school friends retired, we linked up again. Now we do things together. It is like old times. We still talk about school—war stories, mostly—but we have found new activities in which to enjoy one another.

Friendships from earlier in life that are carried into retirement are treasured, but they run their own course. Retirees report that time with old friends is often reduced by new priorities.

Madison   How the time flies in retirement! I thought I would have more time for friends, but I find more clock hours are consumed by visits to distant children and grandchildren and/or babysitting of grandchildren located nearby. Birthday parties, soccer matches, and holiday gatherings fill calendar spaces I thought would be available for long-time friends.

Ethan   I see my old friends every now and then. We are not trying to avoid one another. It seems our schedules don't jibe as easily with more short vacations, longer trips abroad, and part-time work. Some friends moved permanently to other states. When they come back to this area, they are so busy with family that we spend relatively little time with each other.

The type, quality, and number of friendships shift as a result. When long-held friends see each other only once or twice a year, coming together is more like a class reunion where old memories and new family photos are shared before each goes his or her way again.

Judi   The other night, thirteen people—all retired now—by some miracle got together for the first time in years. We first met as couples in the new member class at church, socialized together often, and saw our children grow up and eventually graduate. Two topics dominated our conversation: health-related issues and grandchildren. By the end of the evening, we were recalling how we had met our life's partner. All stories we had heard many years before but seemed to bear repeating after years of absence. Many of our once-common interests were never discussed, like jobs, house repairs, politics, school activities, and religious beliefs. I know we still enjoy and love each other, but my sense is that we all are in different phases of life and have moved on. The social dynamics are no longer the same.

With advancing years come health problems that make it more difficult to meet, mix, and bond with new people. Friendship requires more effort and patience.

Harry   When I gave up my car, my social life took a nosedive. Getting to places is no longer a routine undertaking. Bus and taxi entail advance telephone calls and added expense. Repeatedly asking to ride with others is embarrassing to me and an imposition on their time. I don't want to become a nuisance.

Chloe   Even with a hearing aid, I have problems hearing what people say. Group situations are especially vexing. Room sounds make it difficult for me to understand what the person next to me is saying, much less across the table.

Aaron   I used to be able to remember new names easily. That isn't the case any more. When I meet someone new one week and the next time can't remember his or her name, it is downright embarrassing.

Kyle   Working the crowd used to be my specialty. My wife and I used to ask one another how many people we talked to during the course of a reception. No longer will my unsteady legs get me from point A to point B. Seems like a little thing, but it really cuts down on my contacts with people and staying in touch.

Memories of old friends remain strong, but opportunities to see them diminish with advancing years. Older retirees make this point.

Marie   When I go to a group function expecting to see some old friends, I get the word that this one is ill, that one is homebound, or yet another could not find transportation. Many old friends spend much of the year in a different climate or with distant family members. I really miss their handshakes, hugs, laughter, and glow of conversation.

Jessie   I find myself in retirement eagerly seeking and looking forward to opportunities to mix with people. I value regularly scheduled lunches. Doctor appointments are big calendar days. They address my health concerns and provide human contact. A major highlight in our housing complex is waiting outside the door to see the annual Halloween parade by schoolchildren, and the annual visit by Christmas carolers from the local church.

Christopher   Funerals have become special occasions in my life. They draw people I have known over the years. Respect is paid to the deceased. Sympathy is expressed to loved ones, and the short reception allows for greetings and short conversations with people I rarely see anymore. Even a nod of the head in the distance is a special sign, a reminder that I am yet recognized and remembered. It seems to me that funerals uplift the dignity of the departed and restore the dignity of the living.

Because changes among friends, old and new, are inevitable, making new friends in retirement becomes an absolute necessity. Otherwise, isolation and loneliness will take up permanent residence.

Irene   I never thought much about friendships in my youth and during my working years. They just came and went. Socializing was part of my daily life, almost an afterthought. However, in retirement I no longer take friends for granted. I struggle to find ways and means of being with old friends and I must actively cultivate new friendships. Much of my work in retirement is to fill my social calendar, something that rarely crossed my mind while working full time.

Jack   My son asks me why I go to so many group functions at church and the community center. The answer is simple. Those are the only places where I can meet people of my own age and have fellowship not connected to family. I love my children and grandchildren, but it is important to me to maintain a life aside from them. Otherwise, I might become too much of a burden.

Stewart   The most practical advice I got about friendship came from a speaker at one of our opening school workshops. The speaker, a psychologist from a medical school, gave ten tips how to survive in a changing world. I can only remember his first and last points. The first was not to drive after 10:00 P.M. because that is when the drunks are on the road—humorous except for the reality it bespoke.

   He concluded with this absolute truth: Life is a constant good-bye and hello. Friends move away. Jobs disappear. Businesses fail. Farms consolidate. Companies merge. Governments fall. People die. The reality is that people around us are in constant flux, leaving us alone and isolated unless we make good on the hello possibilities in life. He urged us to greet someone new every day, to find something new about an old friend, or to compliment at least one person close at hand because that forces us to observe them closely and enjoy their uniqueness more.

Gabrielle   My body may be older, but I work to keep my mind sharp. I read daily newspapers and weekly magazines. I surf the Internet. I attend lectures and even listen to some of the new music groups. I don't have any choice if I want friends among the younger generation. Friendship doesn't go very far when the only topic of conversation is past history and health.

Rebecca   I have this important goal in my relationships. Meet new people so my use of the word "we" has one more person in it every day.

LOSING A LIFE PARTNER

All married partners return to single status sooner or later. The shock is profound and becomes a most dreaded retirement transition. For many retirees, it is the first time to live alone.

Hunter   When my wife died, it was the first time in my whole life without another human being close at hand. As a child, I had brothers and sisters. In college, I had a roommate. Prior to marriage, I shared an apartment with another teacher. I took too much for granted in the comfort found in ordinary eye contact, a spoken word, a touch, or an attentive ear.

Carmen   The big house had to go. Too many memories there for me when my husband died. It was like a large museum. Besides, I couldn't keep up the outside and inside. I figured a small townhouse or condominium would better meet my needs and give me a fresh start. Being alone in a smaller space is very different from a big one.

The hardship most often named by the survivor is not aloneness, but loneliness. The heart breaks not once, but over and over again. Fond memories can bring delight, and they can also cast dark shadows on the present.

Elsa   My nights are so long. No longer in the picture is my love. He helped me plan for the day's activities, shared doing them, or listened in the evening to the unfolding. Yes, that dear face can be brought to mind by a single word, a special song, or some commonplace action like lighting a candle or buying a book. I think grief has its own signature for every person.

Iris   If it had not been for my children and grandchildren, I would have perished. When my husband of fifty-five years died, I felt surrounded by their love. I spent much time at their homes until the family home could be sold. I now live in a condo where other people live who have also lost their mates. I can see my husband in the faces of my loved ones and some of the same behaviors, too. I miss him. He would be so proud of his legacy.

Some retirees talk openly about the inevitable end. Others spend minimal time on this hard subject or avoid it altogether.

Alexandria   My husband and I did not dwell on death, but we were very conscientious about end times. We made our health declarations and put them into the right hands. We made estate and funeral plans in advance. Most importantly, we expressed our daily love for each other and did not sidestep what we thought the remaining partner should do about a whole range of things, such as housing, investments, and even seeking a new mate. Every one of these considerations turned out to be a kindness to me in my hours of grief.

Ryan   I did not face the reality and finality of death until my sudden heart attack. Of course, my wife and I visited dying friends in the hospital and attended their funerals, but we did not seriously discuss these matters for ourselves. Pains in my chest and open-heart surgery had the effect of opening my mind also. I began to share estate matters with her more fully, and we have decided to move to a townhouse where she (or I) can live comfortably alone and with no outdoor work responsibilities.

Anna   The police car in our driveway frightened me. I was expecting my husband to come home any minute. He died in a head-on crash. I wasn't prepared in any respect. Our health had been good. We traveled. We visited our children in other states regularly. My husband paid the bills. I took care of the social calendar. Life was good! Suddenly everything descended on me, alone. My name wasn't on the checking and saving accounts, nor was it on our bank safety deposit box. The money and official papers were frozen and locked away. We hadn't discussed cremation or cemetery lots. Decision after decision had to be made when our house was full of visiting friends and family members coming from out of town. It was all too much for me. The overload continued until the estate finally closed two years later.

Newly single persons do report one significant, unexpected, but understandable change. Singleness alters relationships with people who still have their mates.

Simon   When my wife died from cancer, I soon learned in social situations that I and me is very different than we and us. Two is companionship, four is an even pair, and three is an odd number. So are the numbers five, seven, nine, and eleven when long-married couples come together and one has lost a spouse. Also, little signs of affection or deference that persons in partnership share with each other in group situations are like sharp jabs to the widower. As time goes by, I find myself less in the company of other married couples and more in company with other single men. This comes about partly because I am no longer invited to certain social functions where couples gather and partly by my choice because I feel more and more like an outsider, even in the midst of long-time married friends.

Maxine   When couples gather, I think my widow status prompts extra consideration, generates more caution, and reduces the free flow of conversation. By lot and by choice, I find myself linking up more with other single women or going to group functions where I know several single women will also be in attendance.

New loves during retirement bring great rewards as well as some special challenges to relationships. Some hesitate, or even back away from, another marriage while others report delight, companionship, and encouragement to overcome all obstacles.

Shannon   I so enjoy a man's company, but so do most of my female friends. In every one of my social groups, except a country club to which I belong, women outnumber men. I liked the odds in romance better the first time around.

Sheldon   I started dating again some months after my wife died. I quickly detected coolness in conversations with my children. It was like an elephant was in the room. I haven't really addressed it because I'm not serious with anyone. I don't know if they think I am being disloyal to their mother or are worried about the estate if I marry again.

Leroy   My wife passed away three years ago. I retired as a principal shortly thereafter. I wasn't looking for another mate, exactly, but I find women bring something to conversations that men lack. This was especially true of one my wife's friends, a widow, whom I had known for a long time. When Cupid fired his arrow, we both talked to our children. We assured them that our respective estates would stay with original family members and noted that our eagerness for marriage the second time spoke volumes about our first marriages. They gave their blessings and filled the small chapel with grandchildren. One thing we both know is that in our second marriage we are not waiting around to go places or do things that once were put on the shelf for later.

Cheryl   No, I do not have a special male friend or a prospect in mind—but that doesn't mean I'm not looking. I am living testimony that fantasies about companionship, intimacy, and sex don't end at age fifty or sixty or seventy-five. Maybe I will be one of those stories you read about now and then of two older persons finding love. Hope so!

MY JOURNEY

The first six months of retirement were hardest for me. I missed the greetings of the front office receptionist, the flow of people in and out of the office, and meetings wherein people discussed, often debated, and ultimately decided courses of action. By contrast, as a part-time consultant, I sat alone in my home-basement office in front of a computer, hour after hour, composing letters, creating flyers, and addressing family farm fiscal matters. I wasn't in a jail cell, but the isolation often felt like it.

I found it necessary, and helpful, to join a men's Bible study once a week, to go early and remain after Rotary Club meetings, and to eat supper in a restaurant with husbands whose wives were in a social gathering of their own. Consciously seeking out or creating people interaction opportunities now competed with the drive to complete tasks. No longer did the two come together, automatically, within one package. As my part-time consultant business picked up and people interactions increased, I felt more like . . . "happy days are here again."

CONCLUSION

Relationships are a powerful component in all human affairs. In the book *Tuesdays with Morrie* (1997), teacher Morrie, who is dying from Lou Gehrig's disease, shares this insight with Mitch Albom, his former student, now a weekly visitor and chronicler: "In the beginning of life, when we are infants, we need others to survive, right? And at the end of life, when you get like me, you need others to survive, right?" His voice dropped to a whisper. "But here's the secret: in between, we need others as well." This primacy of relationships is readily apparent in all of life and continues into retirement years:

- Life begins in the midst of an intimate male and female relationship.
- Babies cannot survive without relationships; their dependency is total.
- Infants react to relationships; they smile, cry, reach, seek, and suck.
- Children learn through relationships and develop language, habits, and attitudes.
- Pupils spend long hours in relationships in buses, hallways, and classrooms.
- Students are encouraged to develop relationships through cocurricular activities.
- Adolescents yearn for peer relationships; minutes on the phone turn into hours.
- Teenagers thrive on relationships, sometimes in cliques and gangs.
- Young adults commit to relationships; they date, marry, and mate.
- Family members celebrate relationships: birthdays, baptisms, and anniversaries.
- Working adults formalize relationships: partnerships, corporations, unions, management, specialized divisions, departments, and sections.

- Healthy adults create relationships: clubs, associations, and loves.
- Older adults relish relationships: They dote on grandchildren and they congregate together at churches and residential buildings, within tour groups, and in warmer climates.
- Seniors visit lifelong friends in hospitals and attend funerals, and, finally, they bury bodies next to one another, thereby revealing that relationships are a central element in every aspect of life, even unto death.

QUESTIONS TO PONDER OR DISCUSS:

1. What school relationships will you most miss when you retire?
2. To what extent do you think retirement will affect your self-esteem? Why?
3. In what ways will your retirement change domestic relationships? How much attention have you paid to this possibility?
4. Family issues like older parents or new grandchildren can bring surprise and unintended consequences to retirement plans. How much thought have you given these possibilities?
5. What efforts are you making to find new friends even as you say good-bye to old friends?
6. How candidly have you discussed and addressed end times and all attendant relationship issues?

CHAPTER FOURTEEN

Selecting Residence(s)

Many educators move to a new dwelling place at retirement or soon there-after. Most geographical restrictions that are associated with the workplace end with retirement. Fetters fall; the freedom to choose a different residence is at an all-time high.

Charlotte   When my husband and I became eligible for retirement, we took stock. Our children lived in other states. The house was nearly paid off. The neighborhood had changed with younger families moving in. Interest rates were low, and home sales were booming. We asked ourselves where we would most like to live, if not here.

Irwin   The first thing on our agenda when we retired was to move. We told ourselves that when the last day of work ended, we would be heading out as soon as our house sold. We wanted to go someplace where golf could be played year around. Arkansas was our first choice. We had vacationed there many times and found the temperatures to be neither too cold in winter nor extremely hot in summer. Our home now is near the ninth tee on a beautiful golf course. Arkansas is also "Middle America" for convenience of visiting family and friends.

Rosalie   The other day one of my friends handed me a new magazine enti-tled *Places to Retire in Canada*. This was perfect timing. My husband and I own a hobby farm in the country and breed dogs. Suburbia now surrounds our farm, escalating its value and restricting what we can do on the property. For years we talked about selling and moving, but we decided to stick it out until retirement. Our time has come.

ONE, TWO, OR THREE HOMES

The most elemental decision many educators face is the number of places in which to live at one time. If finances permit, it is not unusual to live in one, two, or three places in the course of a year.

Randy   Yes, I remain busy, mostly fixing things. We live in our family home several months each summer, in our retirement home in the South each winter, and in our large recreation vehicle whenever we want to hit the road. Living in three homes gives me plenty to do.

Missy   My parents owned a lake cabin when I was growing up. When my folks died, they left the lake place to me. My husband and I winterized it so we can spend as much time there as we want any time of year. We still have our city home and also rent a place each winter in Texas.

Vern   My sister moved to Arizona after she retired. We visited her several times and decided it would be a good place to live, except in the hot, dry summer months. We sold our family home, bought a place not too far from my sister. In the summer, we return north and live in a trailer home on our lake property that is not too far from our friends and other family members.

CHANGING TYPES OF RESIDENCES

Few retirees live in one dwelling throughout their retirement years. Quite common, in fact, is a gradual transition from one type of dwelling to another. Long-range planning in this regard can be definitive or be left to fate. However, most retirees report making decisions before new circumstances force a move. Keeping control of one's own destiny goes to the heart of dignity and worth.

Wally   I always tried to look ahead as a school business manager and do the right thing before a crisis arose. When we first retired, we sold our older family home, purchased a fifth-wheel recreation vehicle to travel around the United States, and returned to our lake home for the summer months. Later, when we tired of travel, we bought a condo fairly close to downtown so we had good access to theaters, sporting events, and walkways in parks. We now live in a large retirement center operated by the Masons. They have independent living quarters where we now live, assisted living quarters when health conditions require special services, and facilities for full-time, around-the-clock nursing care if health problems so warrant. This is a final move for us, a responsible thing to do when we can still make good decisions and be in charge of our lives. Too many people wait too long to act.

Shirley   We should have sold our house earlier. It was fine for us as long as we could both navigate the stairs to the bedrooms upstairs. My husband suffered a stroke that left one side of his body partly paralyzed, his speech slurred, and his mind not what it used to be. We kept thinking things would turn around, but they didn't. So I ended up selling the house, buying a one-floor townhouse, and disposing of much furniture and the second car. The housing market was depressed when I had to sell, but I had no other choice than to reduce the price.

Leo   For thirty-five years, my wife and I lived in a ranch-style house that was close to the schools where we worked. It was spacious, had a nice yard, and was perfect for raising kids. We continued to live there in retirement until our son and daughter-in-law had their second child and began looking for a larger home. The timing was perfect. We were ready to downsize. They wanted more space and good schools. They bought our home and we moved to a town-house farther out in the suburbs—close, but not too close to them.

MANY CONSIDERATIONS IN HOME LOCATION

Loved ones are one of the prime considerations in home selection during retirement. Retired educators frequently report that a continued responsibility for older family members or valued roles in the lives of their offspring plays a major role in where they live.

Ralph   I am an only son of divorced parents. Mom raised me and has remained in her three-floor family home until this very day (basement, main floor, and upstairs). Her knees bother her. She is no longer steady on her feet. I fear a fall and the danger of her living alone. Here's my dilemma. As a recent retiree, I'm ready for adventure. But what is the right decision for Mom? I can't just leave her. She doesn't want to move to a senior center and even so, she has always counted on me for conversation, love, and support. If I move away, how will she fare? How will I feel? I am torn up inside.

Mildred   Our three daughters grew up, attended out-of-state colleges, and took jobs in other states. The oldest is married and has three charming children. After our retirement, we sold our home and bought a townhouse near them. One year later, our son-in-law was offered a promotion he couldn't refuse that required a transfer to another state. He accepted the offer, and they moved. Do we move with them, stay, or strike out on our own?

Clarence   Our daughter and her husband bought a home in the same community where we live and where I served my last stint as school superintendent. They both work and have preschool and elementary-age children. When

I retired, my wife and I decided to stay put at least for a few years. We are now the day-care providers and are happy to do it. What better or more important investment to make than in your own grandchildren? When the children are older, we will still have time to move elsewhere if that is our heart's desire.

Ruby   Last night I watched a high school girls' soccer game. Our nine-year-old granddaughter plays soccer, and her team had their turn standing around the perimeter of the field to chase stray balls. She hopes to be playing on the high school field herself a few years hence. So do I move away? What can be better for me than stay right here watching and cheering my grandchildren as they grow up?

Another consideration often mentioned by retirees in home selection is the desire to remain in the same community or to become a part of a new community. Housing choice plays a major role in filling the need to belong.

Elizabeth   I decided to remain right here when I retired seven years ago. I love this neighborhood. Rarely do I buy groceries without seeing someone I know. I belong to Anna Circle in church that gets together monthly for fellowship in member homes. I greet neighbors as old friends, and when their children return for a visit, I get to see them too, and remember the candy, magazines, and Christmas wrapping paper they once peddled at our doorstep. Where else could I go at this time in my life that would fill these warm spots in my heart? Community can't be loaded into a moving truck nor be guaranteed at the other end.

Elmer   During our first year in retirement, my wife and I visited friends who had moved to a Florida condominium. It was beautiful, and they introduced us to many of their new friends. They ate out, went fishing, played cards, saw movies, enjoyed the pool, attended church, and found almost instant community. Others sought their company even as they sought companionship. When a unit became available in the same building, we bought in and three years later have no regrets.

Lynne   My husband and I had very specific criteria for our first retirement home. We wanted a college town not too large or too small in a warm climate. I also hoped to teach French part time. The place needed to have a connecting airport, reasonably priced townhouses, and an active cultural arts program. A small city in Texas turned out to be the perfect choice for us. I did teach. We lived there for twelve and a half years before we moved near my brother in Tennessee for another seven years. My husband died recently. We had many wonderful years together and no regrets.

Ownership of a place to live represents a significant capital investment. Money tied up in property is not available for living expenses and other purposes such as travel or gift giving. In selecting a retirement home, matching financial resources and recognizing cash flow need to be other considerations.

Grant   We purchased our lake home long before city people four hours away began buying up properties for summer residences and retirement homes. Values escalated. The small cabins around us sold at unbelievable high prices, and many new owners tore them down to build huge homes. Each year, the taxes climbed by double-digit numbers and ate us right out of house and home, though we made no significant property improvements. As much as we enjoyed the lake, we sold the property for great profit, reinvested some of the capital in a townhouse, and put the balance into long-term bonds. What we pay in taxes has been greatly reduced. The extra income is also giving us more budget leeway.

Vicki   We sold our neighborhood house for a good price soon after we retired and bought a town home. Why did we leave after thirty-two years? Everything in the house had aged, along with us: windows, furnace, roof, kitchen, bathroom, and appliances. Every dollar we received for the house went to pay for a new townhouse, but everything around us is new again and should work well for the rest of our lives.

Martin   My wife and I started our married life in a small, rural town. I taught and coached. Reluctantly, we moved to the city when an opportunity of a lifetime came to teach and coach at a much higher salary. We promised ourselves we could move back to our roots, so to speak, when we retired. We made good on that promise a year ago. We doubled our money on the sale of our city home, paid cash for a comparably sized rural home for half the price. We invested the leftover cash equity, which helps our cash flow. Our real estate tax has been greatly reduced, and labor costs for home repairs are also less. We see cornfields out our back windows and tend our large flower garden in front. This is the life for us.

OTHER FACTORS IN HOME SELECTION

Maintenance of property is a consideration in home selection. What may have been routine work and even pleasure at one point in life can change during retirement years.

Howard   Our family home had almost everything, including a pool. When our children grew up and left, I could no long count on their help. At the same time, I no longer felt like a spring chicken. Trees in our yard had grown tall. Every storm distributed twigs. Leaves blanketed our yard every fall. Another chore I did with growing reluctance was cleaning and covering the pool. We bought a lovely townhouse not too far away, and I feel like I got my life back.

Olivia   We sold our stand-alone home and bought a townhouse. The monthly payment for maintenance matched our budget and we thought we were all set in our retirement years. What has surprised us the most is the rapid increase in monthly maintenance fees. My husband used to do much of that type of work in our former home, but here it is all contracted out. Everything is neat as a pin and beautiful to behold, but it does come with a price tag.

Elma   Not too long after my husband died, I moved from the home where we raised our children to a condo. I hadn't realized how many fix-up things there were around a house. He did them without complaint, and I never paid much attention until they fell to me. Leaking faucets, rooting out old bushes, replacing light bulbs out of easy reach, exterior painting, resurfacing the driveway, and snow removal are some examples. I was so happy to leave all these things behind.

Major, periodic types of maintenance occur in nearly all types of homes. Anticipation of such one-time expenses is necessary for realistic budget planning.

Hazel   My fourth-floor condo overlooks the Atlantic Ocean. Depending on the breeze direction, I sometimes get salt spray heavily upon my windows and the walkout decks by the kitchen and back bedroom. City inspectors discovered cracks in the deck cement. Over the years, salt spray eroded the steel reinforcement rods, and all decks have had to be replaced. A huge special assessment now faces me.

Erling   We moved into a third-ring suburb when we got married. Commutes were longer, but houses were less expensive. We had our own septic system until last year. A sprawling metropolis now engulfs us. The powers-that-be decided to install a new sewer system, a major expense that we can pay off through installments, in a lump sum now, or when we sell the house.

Clinton   About a year ago, my visiting son-in-law opened a den window to cool the room and came back saying the windowsill had started to rot. When we checked other windows in our forty-five-year-old house, we discovered the same deterioration problem in most of them. Rainwater was going into wall spaces beneath the windows, wetting the insulation. We got bids from several window replacement companies. The cost was about the same as we had paid for the house originally. Needless to say, we were stunned.

Home resale is yet another consideration for potential owners. The three words most often cited regarding property resale are location, location, and location. There are other factors to consider as well, such as the number and types of buyers, marketplace conditions such as interest rates, and family members who can help with sale and relocation.

Emily   We bought a condo in Florida for our retirement home. It had all the amenities we wanted and it served us well until my husband died and I wished to be closer to my children. That is when I took serious note that newer, more attractive condos had been built in the area and that covenants for our building excluded many buyers. The number of showings was much less than I expected. I changed realtors twice before it finally sold.

Arlo   Our rural home sat in a beautiful setting and was larger than most homes in the area. When we listed our home for sale, we expected it to be gobbled up immediately. We were sorely disappointed. More people are moving out of our area than moving in, and the price of our home was not in the ballpark for most homebuyers. After two years, and much distress on our parts, the home finally sold. Ironically, the buyer came from the same city where we wanted to go.

Gwen   My husband and I moved to the Gulf Coast at the end of our careers. It was great for nine years until my husband was diagnosed with a nonma-lignant brain tumor. Doctors operated and saved his life, but he is no longer the same person. He is hanging on by a thread in a nursing home. I want to move closer to my daughter, so she can help me through this terrible time, but our condo won't sell. A recent hurricane damaged property in this area and has scared off new buyers.

Erma   California was where we made our retirement home. That was long ago, before the real estate market went crazy. My husband recently passed away from an intestinal infection that took his life in just three days. I'm in a meltdown state. All of our children currently live in the Midwest and East Coast. My husband handled most of the business side of things. How much is the house worth? How do I select a good realtor? What shall be done with the second car, the furniture, and sailboat? What should be done with the insurance money? Family members came for the funeral but had to return to their jobs and children. If we had elected to live closer to them, they would be able to help shoulder the weight I am carrying.

RETIREES OCCUPY EVERY IMAGINABLE TYPE OF HOME

Educators, like people everywhere, reveal their individuality in the type of homes in which they elect to live during retirement. America presents a myriad of choices.

Deborah   I rented an apartment through my working years and continue to do so in retirement for many reasons. I don't carry a mortgage. I can easily predict my housing costs during the lease period. There is the convenience factor; most apartments have close access to major highways. Rental rates may increase, but I can choose to stay or go. I have always liked the flexibility of a rental unit and still do today.

Connie   How we enjoy the sea! In retirement, we decided to purchase a small home on a bluff overlooking the ocean. It was pricey but we think a good investment. However, we also wanted a place back in the city to keep up our friendships, church membership, and time with family and relatives. Keeping our family home involved just too much upkeep, especially with some outdoor work at our new get-away place. So we sold our house, bought a condominium, divided up our furniture between the two places, and are enjoying the best of both worlds.

Orv   I thoroughly enjoy my townhouse and can live comfortably with the rules in this large development. Not so a new neighbor who is a retired farmer. First, he purchased a flower stand for his entrance area with room for six pots of flowers when townhouse rules limit front-door flowerpots to five. Next, he planted some of his own flowers in the common flower garden and inserted a rusty, old plowshare as an added decoration. He thinks he is still on the farm. I suppose he will be bringing in loads of fresh manure next. I think the board of directors should do its job and enforce the rules. Otherwise, the reputation of our development will hurt future home sales.

Gerald   For years, my wife and I dreamed about playing on golf courses in every state of the union. When we retired, we bought the largest truck made by Dodge and a fifth wheeler to match. We changed our address to North

Dakota where taxes are low and set out on our quest. If we liked a place, we stayed a week or even a month. If we got the itch to move, we were on the road again. Once or twice a year, we left our fifth wheeler parked someplace when we returned to see our children and grandchildren. After three years, we decided to settle down and are now building a house in a Texas community with, you guessed it, many golf courses.

Rod and Audrey   In our first two years into retirement, we left the cold country for a month and rented a townhouse in New Mexico. The rental charge was substantial, but we enjoyed the warmth and new surroundings for a luxurious thirty-one days. But a month didn't seem long enough. We were willing to settle for something more economical to remain longer. A trailer home for sale in the same general area was the right ticket for us because it would be paid for in three years if we applied the townhouse rental check. We now own it outright and can stay as long as we like.

Henry and Arietta   Boats and water have been mainstays in our life ever since we left the dry prairies of North Dakota. In the last years before retirement, we purchased a large cabin cruiser with dual diesel engines, ship-to-shore radio equipment, and everything needed to eat and sleep on board for days or weeks. We moored it on the St. Croix River in Wisconsin and used it like a summer cabin on weekends and holidays. After retirement, we motored down the Mississippi River and spent the first couple of years traveling up and down the coast from New Orleans to Miami and Miami to New York and back again. We sold the big boat three months ago, but don't be surprised if we buy another one. We now live in a year-round home on a lake in central Minnesota, but the draw of the sea still tempts us.

Jerry and Lois   Our kids are grown and scattered. We want to help our children stay in touch with one other and our grandchildren (the cousins) to meet and learn to love one another, too. We bought a time-share unit in Louisiana on the Gulf Coast where we all meet at the same time every year. We know far in advance about the dates, and we use some of our retirement money to help them with transportation costs. It is crowded with babies, toddlers, and school-age children. Such mayhem, but we all love it and return the next year.

Willis   We lived in five different homes during our married life. All were built by other people. We began talking about building our dream home about five years before our retirement. We followed the Parade of Homes, shopped in upscale furniture stores, and signed up for magazines that covered everything from floor designs to interior decorations and landscaping. We found an architect we liked and visited homes constructed by a builder whom we eventually selected. More difficult was finding the right lot for what we had in mind. Our dream home is nearing completion, and we can't wait to move in, get settled, and have a big housewarming for our friends.

MY JOURNEY

During my career, we lived in many different locations: Minnesota, Michigan, Indiana, Japan, and Illinois. I traveled as a consultant to twenty-four different states. We vacationed throughout the United States and several foreign countries. We also lived or spent considerable time in many different dwellings: apartments, campus housing, end-of-tool shed, leased homes, a starter home, an older fix-up home, hotels, resorts, tents, a camper, cabins, and a remodeled barn (for guests). On one trip across the country, we slept in the back of a pick-up truck under the stars. Our itch to travel has been well scratched, and we've learned that home is wherever you and loved ones nest together.

The bottom line for us is not one community but many: (1) We enjoy city, lake, and farm communities because we know a host of people and they know us; (2) We appreciate our church community and the opportunities to serve and be served; and (3) We love our family, our nuclear community, which now includes grandchildren who live near us. We never want to be apart from them for very long.

CONCLUSION

Adults often refer to their residence as their home. In a functional sense, an apartment, house, or townhouse is the means by which basic human needs such as rest, sustenance, intimacy, procreation, and sanctuary are met. Home is a gathering place, a being place, a connecting place, a private place, and a protected space in which many facades fall and our humanness can show and still be accepted. Retirees discover that residences can change, but that what we call home stays much the same because that is who we are when the world is shut out.

However, retirees also learn that residences are structures that are located almost anywhere, take every form and shape, and utilize a multitude of construction materials. As such, retirees point out that selection of a dwelling place is a major decision because so many life variables are determined by that decision:

- Likely neighbors and possible friendships.
- Proximity to family.
- Closeness to shopping, worship center, alternative transportation.
- Use of capital resources and investment strategy.
- Recreation possibilities.
- Safety, status, and reputation.
- Length of stay, particularly in the face of handicapping conditions that may come.

QUESTIONS TO PONDER OR DISCUSS:

1. How seriously have you considered a different place to live after you retire? What holds you back in these conversations? What encourages you to continue them?
2. How different or similar will your retirement dwelling place(s) be from where you now live?
3. Among your friends and associates, who have already moved into their retirement home? What prompted their decisions? To what extent do you agree with their explanations?
4. What are the primary considerations in selecting your next living place?
5. What changes do you see in your living places and spaces in coming years?
6. How do you know when the time is right to make a move?

CHAPTER FIFTEEN

Preparing for Health Challenges

Good health enables; poor health restricts. All retirees want the former and worry about the latter. No aspect of retirement is more certain than changes in the human body that reflect decades of use. The transitions caused by health issues are among the most challenging in the whole of life.

Victor   Our financial planner told us not to wait until later to fulfill our travel dreams. He said the first ten years following retirement are usually good health years. Thereafter, one or the other partner often has a medical condition that prevents distant travel.

Lorna   My husband retired after thirty-eight years of teaching. Our journey with his Parkinson's disease for eighteen years has been difficult. This past year was another deep valley experience when he broke his neck and was under intensive medical care for many months. It pushed our patience, pocketbook, and faith.

Alice   Heart problems have been in my family (father's side) for generations. My high blood pressure has been controlled thus far by a healthy lifestyle. My doctor requires me to have regular check-ups. I hold my breath each time we talk during an office visit.

Lisa   I am on the prayer chain at church. Medical problems of people clearly dominate the list of prayer requests. I am now conscious that so many prayers involve people who are older because I, too, have moved into that age group. On forms listing age groupings, I now check the last category.

GOOD HEALTH HABITS

Preventative steps best serve long-term health interests. Among those recommended by physicians almost universally are regular exercise, good diet, adequate rest, and proactive medical care. A positive attitude plays a major role also in maintaining good health and recovering from ill health.

Allen   I was a three-season athlete in high school and college. I could eat like a horse and still stay thin. This high exercise lifestyle continued for many years as a coach and avid tennis player. As my family matured and my energy level began to taper off, I gave up all but one coaching assignment and switched from tennis to golf. My doctor expressed alarm at the weight gain and recommended a combination of a good diet and more rigorous and regular exercise. I did lose a few pounds and my ongoing goal is to build regular exercise into my weekly schedule.

Aretha   Weight became a problem for me after the birth of our third child. I never regained my prebirth weight and I lost more ground with each advancing year. A routine physical brought me up short. My doctor bluntly said, "Your heart is under tremendous strain. It has enlarged." He urged me to take charge of my diet to deter a high probability of a stroke and other health problems. This is easier said than done but I know he is right and I owe it to my family and myself to follow through.

Kyle   When a child, I had difficulty sitting still for even short periods of time. My energy levels kept me in constant motion. I was restless at night. The slightest noise would awaken me. Today, I would probably be diagnosed as a case of attention deficit disorder. Through my working years, I rarely got more than six hours of sleep a night. Now my doctor recommends a short nap after noon lunch, noting that six hours of rest a night are too few for a man my age.

Millie   When we retired, we consciously changed our eating habits. This watershed time in our life made us aware that diet may well determine how many healthful years we have left. We read some good books on nutrition. We now eat more meals at home and take more time to buy, prepare, and eat the right foods. We also work out regularly at a health club. We have lost some weight and feel good.

Lewis   During my working years I often became ill right after the completion of a major project like a school referendum that had sapped my energy, reduced hours of sleep, altered eating habits, and drained my spirit. In retirement, I am trying to maintain a better balance in all aspects of healthful living. I want to give myself a fighting chance when the flu bugs come my way.

Retirees who are health conscious also take precautionary steps to avoid abuse to mind and body. For example, too much sun, tobacco use, excessive alcohol consumption, and the use of illicit drugs or wrongfully used prescription drugs are serious health risks recognized by health-conscious seniors.

Loren Five years ago, a pimple on my nose would not heal. A skin specialist determined it was basal cell carcinoma, a form of skin cancer that is rarely fatal. He said my bucket of sun was filled early in life (I was an outdoor farm boy), told me to stay under wraps henceforth, and to put on a facial skin cream daily. Removing the spot on my nose hurt like hell. You should see all the hats in my closet these days. I do wear them!

Haley Migraine headaches were my bane throughout my career, but they came much more often when I served as superintendent. My doctor said inordinate amounts of tension increase the risk of migraines. I believed him and got out.

Nils My hearing loss became noticeable the last six or seven years prior to retirement. I denied the problem at first, but my family's complaints about the loud TV and my own awareness of saying "What?" more often finally got me to the doctor. The loss was greater in one ear than the other, but hearing aids were prescribed for both. The prescription included wearing earplugs when I use the chain saw or other loud equipment, mow the lawn, or attend a noisy game or concert. My goals are to avoid loud sounds that exacerbate my hearing loss and to purchase new hearing aids when new technological advances will improve what I can hear.

Gale I am a recovering alcoholic. An intervention meeting midcareer that included coworkers and family members sent me into treatment. There wasn't any family history that I know about, so I remained in denial for a long time. Finally, with ongoing help from AA, I openly admit I am vulnerable to this health problem and can never take another drink. In retirement, I spend more time alone so the temptation to drink is greater now than when I was so busy with work. Now I attend two support groups instead of one.

Mel In my wife's case, just one drink had become two, and two had become three until her meds got all out of whack. Her thinking lost coherence. She was showing strange, even bizarre, behavior that landed her in the hospital. We now know that senior citizens are as vulnerable to dependency behavior as anyone else. Maybe more so, because health issues related to age often prompt more pill prescriptions, and too much time spent alone can make alcohol look like a friend.

MEDICAL CARE

Expert medical advice is needed throughout life but is sought more frequently with advancing age. Incidences of ill health or lack of good medical attention accumulate over the years. Awareness grows that life itself often hangs in the balance. This new realization, in turn, prompts a heightened concern for the availability and quality of medical care.

John   I went to the doctor's office a couple of weeks ago, and I was asked to complete a one-page form asking my home address, insurance coverage, past medical history, and current use of drugs and vitamins. I thought to myself, "All that information is already included in the three-and-a-half-inch folder with my name. Doesn't anyone ever read it?" Then the doctor, all businesslike, came in, asked me to describe my ailment, looked down the one-page sheet, made a quick diagnosis, wrote a prescription that I could not read, and was ready to exit when I interrupted with probing questions. I felt the cold in that exam room on my skin and in my heart. I drove home muttering: "If this is how I'm treated at age sixty-six when I have all my faculties and can advocate for myself, what will be my fate when I am older, more infirm, and possibly less bold?"

Marl   I turned sixty-seven a month ago. Since my birthday, I have been to a doctor's office six times: eye exam, hearing aid repair, teeth cleaning, annual skin cancer check-up, numb hands at night (possible carpel tunnel), and, can you believe it, jock itch. Thankfully, no life-threatening situation prompted these visits. I do seem to see doctors more often the older I get.

Shelly   We sold our summer cabin after thirty-five years of enjoyment. Since my heart attack, I just don't feel comfortable spending time in the deep woods so far from medical help. My husband doesn't want to leave me alone in the city, so we agreed the best thing to do was to sell our cabin while everything still worked and looked good.

Kevin   About three years ago, a retired friend had a routine physical. The doctor found colon cancer. There had been no sign of it one year earlier. Having caught it early, my friend had surgery and follow-up treatment; his doctors think at this point he can live a normal life span. My friend is an important object lesson to me. I now put a thorough physical exam first thing on my New Year's calendar.

Marvel   I love my high school class reunions, but one segment in the evening program makes me sad; that is reading the names of deceased classmates.

When I make inquiry about those I'd lost track of, I hear about health problems I never even imagined in my youth and during most of my career years. The next reunion will be our fiftieth, and, I suppose, more of the same.

Del   Finding good medical care is now a major concern for us. When we moved to Colorado to be closer to our daughter's family, we learned that many doctors in the Denver area are willing to continue serving long-term patients who have since become eligible for Medicare, but they will not accept new Medicare patients because authorized payments are too far below their regular billings. We found ourselves going to one office after another. Rejections are a new, scary phenomenon to us.

Esther   Placing my husband into a nursing home was the hardest thing I ever did in married life. Alzheimer's had advanced to the point where he would leave the house and wander aimlessly throughout the neighborhood. Also, his ability to communicate and take care of his bodily functions gradually slipped away. I could not control or lift him. Out of exhaustion and desperation, I had no other option. Then more medical questions faced me. What facilities are available? Would good medical care be provided? How much can I afford? How long will he live? Questions like these came at me at the very time I was least prepared physically and emotionally to answer them.

INSURANCE COVERAGE

Health insurance is expensive but the financial vulnerability without it is even worse. Knowing this fact, retirees explore health insurance options carefully prior to and following retirement and learn that health insurance is seldom addressed by one source.

Roger   My school district held a meeting for all retiring employees to acquaint us with insurance options. A new set of circumstances faced my wife and me. We planned a move out-of-state for a major portion of each year and our current health policy selection required treatment at clinics located within the geographic area where I worked. We had to make a change in our insurance plan that would protect us medically, both home and away.

Felicia   I'm worried about health coverage in my retirement. I know older people are more prone to health problems. My income is fixed. I am paying the full freight for health premiums. Horror stories about escalating prescription drug costs frighten me. Even though my budget will be stretched, I decided to take maximum medical coverage to age sixty-five, at which time I will become eligible for Medicare. Thereafter, more decisions face me, because many types of supplemental health insurance plans are in the marketplace. I have never liked making health insurance decisions.

Many school districts offer their employees dental coverage or partial payment toward dental insurance coverage. What happens to dental coverage at the time of retirement? Should dental insurance be continued when it becomes pay-as-you go? These are also health-related questions.

Ralph   One of my retirement decisions was whether or not to continue in the school dental insurance program. The full premium cost would have to be born by me. The school group rates include younger families with children so adverse selection in the insurance pool had to be considered. One trip to the dentist helped me make a decision. An aging cap on a molar needed to be replaced. I was astounded at the current cost compared to the cost thirty-five years ago. Even though insurance only covers a portion of cap replacement, I have a mouthful of caps and decided to retain the dental insurance policy into retirement.

Andreas   When I studied the dental insurance plan offered through the district for retirees, I learned the patient must pay the first several hundred dollars of costs before the policy kicks in. In effect, the insurance policy covers only the most severe dental problems. My own dental history, and that of my family, has been particularly good, so I declined the dental insurance options and follow the pay-as-you-go plan (self-funding). So far, so good.

Advances in medical care can prolong life, and the probability that some of this time will be spent in a nursing home increases, too. This fact prompts the most rapidly growing sector of the insurance industry, that of long-term care insurance. Twenty-first-century retirement transitions include investigation of such policies and all the related decisions.

Alvin and Frances   Our financial planner noted that our estate would serve us well in retirement as long as we were both healthy, but what if one or both of us required nursing home care? Even a sizable estate can go to zero in a hurry with those phenomenal costs. He recommended we consider long-term care insurance. By the time we got around to it, we had already retired and found the annual premiums to be very high relative to our income. If we had purchased the same policy at an earlier age, we would not be so burdened.

Marge and Denny   Picking the right insurance company to carry our long-term health insurance was a challenge. We didn't want the company to go bankrupt about the time we might need their payout. Nor did we want the company to unduly increase the annual premium amounts since our income is relatively fixed. In the first case, we learned that our state (not true in all states) has an emergency fund for insurance companies that cannot meet their commitments. In the second case, we learned that some companies have long track records and others do not. Some have lower premiums at the outset but greater increases later. The decision to purchase long-term care insurance was easy for us, but not who should be the carrier.

Nancy   I am a widow with a small nest egg. I don't want my children to be worried about me. Long-term care insurance gives me peace of mind and, I trust, them, too. What took my time in decision making were the questions pertaining to the extent of coverage, which has a tremendous impact on annual premium payments. Did I want the policy to provide high, medium, or low daily payments? Did I want the policy to make the period of coverage to be one year, two years, three years, or unlimited? The probability tables show that the average long-term care is about two years and is going down gradually. However, I also learned that such statistics can be misleading. These averages usually include patients who are quickly released from hospitals following surgery and who need transition care—a place with nursing services for an extended period of recuperation.

Cassandra   My husband and I looked into long-term care insurance but decided against it. He has been very successful in business. Our net worth is considerable, more than sufficient to cover any long-term care expenses either of us may have. Businesses fail, however, so I am not completely sold on our decision, but my husband says not to worry.

One aspect of health insurance that comes from retirees throughout America is the tremendous increase in associated paperwork. Seldom does experience prior to retirement fully prepare the retiree for what follows.

Heather   When Medicare kicked in for my husband and me, the paper shuffle involving insurance moved into big time. The doctor's office sends the bill to the Medicare people who pay a portion of the bill and (usually, but not always) send their decision to the doctor, the supplemental insurance company, and me. In turn, the supplemental insurance company decides how much of the balance they will pay and so informs the doctor's office and me. Sometimes there is patient pay left on the bill. Believe me! What I've just described is oversimplified. Before one doctor's bill is settled, we usually have additional office visits, so tracking what insurance policies are paying and what is left for direct payment becomes very difficult.

Ellyn   My doctor once sent me an itemized bill that was three single-spaced pages in length. It covered a twelve-month period. One item on the list, that I was supposed to pay directly, was ten months old and was on the list for the very first time. When I called the clinic and complained about the protracted delay in billing, I was told not to pay it because some law requires speedier notification. Why was I not surprised to see it listed again on my next bill?

Brett   When my doctor sends lab work for analysis to an outside network-company, they usually bill me directly, oblivious to my multiple insurance coverage (Medicare and supplemental insurance). This starts a new round of telephone calls and correspondence. It usually gets straightened out in due time, but it can be quite a headache.

LIVING QUARTERS

Health and wellness play a major role in retirement housing decisions (see chapter 14). Health considerations early in retirement may prompt one decision and yet another later in retirement. Clearly, aging brings issues of mind and body into the mix of choices related to living quarters.

Damon   Taking care of two places, our family home and summer cabin, got to be too much upkeep. I tire more easily these days and do not want to work all the time. We sold the family home, bought a townhouse, and deeded the lake place to our children.

Cynthia   When we moved to Florida, we bought a home without a basement. Everything was on the same floor, and we decided never again to have a house with multiple floors. Our knees just are not what they used to be.

Lowell   We just sold our family home because it was too big (too much cleaning) and had no bedroom on the main floor. When my wife was recovering from hip surgery, I made countless trips up and down the steps. Never again! We are moving into a condo with elevators that is located within walking access to all the stores we need, as well as the doctor's office.

Bernice   When my husband died, I was left with all the yard work, snow shoveling, lawn mowing, hedge trimming, and so forth. I never liked that kind of work. In any case, I just am not up to it anymore. I sold the house and rented a nice apartment not too far from my daughter.

Clementine   My husband is terminally ill. I am his caregiver within our family home. When he dies, who will take care of me? That troubling question prompted me to put my name on the list for a church-related senior citizen facility with three types of housing: independent living, assisted living, and skilled-care living. When an independent living apartment opens up, I will sell this house and join many of my friends who are already living there.

FINAL WISHES

End times do come. Some early, some late, but invariably all retirees move into that last stage of life, like long-distance runners who approach the finish line. In this anchor run, serious health issues and final wishes are addressed by design or default. No one can predict their time of arrival, so most retirees undertake making final wishes known while still in optimum health. Those with plans in place comment that it is an act of love to tell others what you wish to be done so they are not conflicted about courses of action.

Carol   My brother is an attorney specializing in estate matters. Based upon his experience, he urged my husband and me to make a living will and provided us with forms. Each of us was able to state what we wished would happen if a health condition required decisions that we could not make for ourselves. We both decided against medical life support when all semblance of a good quality life is no longer a possibility. Also, we were asked about organ donation and other pertinent matters, such as who is authorized to act on our behalf.

Samson   My wife was rushed by ambulance to the hospital following a terrible car accident. I was told her head injuries were so severe that all hope for recovery was gone and that her coma would persist indefinitely as long as artificial life support was continued. I discussed with our children whether or not to remove life support but the living will signed by my wife much earlier told us her wishes. We honored them. She died peacefully. We, too, are at peace.

Laurie   My husband and I learned the hard way that it is not enough to sign a living will telling loved ones your health wishes when the end is near. You must make signed copies available to the doctor, children, pastor, and whoever else might be involved when you are no longer in charge of your faculties. My father told me he had a living will but no one, including Mother, could find the copy when he had a serious stroke.

Maurice   The exercise of completing a living will did much more for me than reflect my last wishes relative to health deterioration. It got me to thinking who I should thank and from whom I should seek forgiveness. We never know when the Lord will call us home. Leaving unfinished business isn't good stewardship. When I took care of these matters, my heart was much more peaceful.

A final will and testament is the way a person tells survivors about final wishes regarding the estate (see chapter 12). Sometimes these wishes are also recorded within a trust. If the deceased does not specify the estate administrator and the beneficiaries in a legal document, the government will do so in accordance with established state laws. One way or another, assets are distributed.

Craig   Money talks in life. Money talks in death also. The departed loved one signals his or her values by how an estate is distributed. I attended the reading of the will of a friend whose father left all but one dollar to one son and nothing but that one dollar to the other son. This obvious show of favoritism reflected what I saw in life, too, causing much enmity between the brothers.

Colleen   While our mother was seriously ill in the hospital, my three sisters and I got together to encourage and support her and to discuss next-stage issues under three scenarios (fully recovers, partially recovers, or dies). At night, we all slept in the family home so we had adequate time to see and talk about family heirlooms. There were obvious conflicts but no heated arguments. (The whole business was distasteful with Mother's future so uncertain.) When Mother died and the will was read, thank goodness everything was laid out regarding who was to receive what. We were spared rivalry that could have hurt our deep affection for one another.

Gale   My father called all five children to his bedside some days before his passing. He told us how much he loved each one of us. He expressed gratitude for a long life with good health and a loving family. Last, he prayed that his earthly goods would be distributed without rancor and he told us we would each receive a 15 percent share and that the remaining 10 percent and 15 percent would go respectively to church and charities. That is exactly what we later read in his will. Healthy relationships are what he most wanted to preserve. He paraphrased from the Bible that a person with everything but not love, truly has nothing.

MY JOURNEY

I often think of my four grandparents and parents in their older ages, all of whom lived long lives, so I observed changes in their health. My dad's dad had such stiff knees at age eighty-five that his legs would not bend at all. He appeared to walk on stilts. Dad, too, had stiff knees and had one knee replaced twice by surgery. A couple of months ago, my knees hurt going up the stairs. I asked my doctor about it. He said, "I see some titanium in your future."

CONCLUSION

Health is the least predictable variable in all of life. In a blink of an eye, a beautiful day of sunshine can turn to dull gray or be filled with a cloudburst of anxiety, hurt, or remorse. Over the passing years, retirees hear horror stories or have personal experiences of pain and suffering that make the vulnerability of human life so very plain.

Simultaneously, other stories remind retirees of miracle drugs, transplants, and life-saving surgery that provide hope. The see-saw effect keeps health issues in the forefront of the brain and prompts close attention to concerns, challenges, and commitments related to health, including the following that come from the National Institute on Aging Information Center, U.S. Department of Health and Human Services, January 2002 (niainfor@jbs1.com):

- Eat a balanced diet, including five helpings of fruits and vegetables a day.
- Exercise regularly (check with a doctor before starting an exercise program).
- Get regular health check-ups.
- Don't smoke (it's never too late to quit).
- Practice safety habits at home to prevent falls and fractures. Always wear your seatbelt in a car.
- Stay in contact with family and friends. Stay active through work, play, and community.
- Avoid overexposure to the sun and the cold.
- If you drink, moderation is the key. When you drink, let someone else drive.

- Keep personal and financial records in order to simplify budgeting and investing. Plan long-term housing and monetary needs.
- Keep a positive attitude toward life. Do things that make you happy.

QUESTIONS TO PONDER OR DISCUSS:

1. What have doctors said to you about the state of your health? What recommendations have come to you about exercise, diet, and rest? Which ones have been followed or not followed? Why?
2. What professional health care providers are available to you now? How confident are you that this same level of health care will be available if you move to a new geographic area?
3. What changes in health plans, if any, are necessary for you to enjoy your retirement life style? Why or why not would the long-term care insurance be a wise choice for you?
4. Who can you turn to for assistance in the event of health problems and/or the associated paperwork?
5. What type of living quarters are an improvement over your present quarters regarding future health complications?
6. What steps have you taken to record and make well known your final wishes regarding health concerns and estate distribution?

ALIGNING VALUE
COMMITMENTS CONSCIOUSLY

Values that draw educators into the profession play themselves out throughout the working years. What motivates, gives direction, and provides reward
to educators most of their lives need not end at retirement. Stories in section
IV illustrate that lifelong values do not end at retirement but often become
manifested in new and extended ways.

Chapter 16 explores definitions of success before and after retirement. The
importance of continuity to belong to community is emphasized in chapter
17. Caring for others forms a bedrock value for professional educators, and
this powerful orientation continues to be a driving force for retirees. This is
described in chapter 18.

Educators often remind students and one another that learning is lifelong.
That principle is amply proven by their actions in their own retirement. Chapter 19 gives many illustrations and enlarges the list of learning options during
retirement years.

Faith is another dimension that is often challenged by circumstances in retirement. Many retirees report serious struggles with the mysteries of living
and dying and a growing, more mature understanding of human nature. Often, but not always, they speak of a renewed faith commitment. This important aspect of life's journey is included in chapter 20.

Defining Success before and after Retirement

The definitions of success prior to and following retirement reveal deeply held values. Some educators express these values easily. Descriptive words flow with comfort. Others struggle to find the words and typically point to activities that reflect the values rather than give them direct expression. Nearly all retirees report that deeply held convictions helped to set directions during working years and continue to set the course in retirement.

Abigail   People are in the center of my circle, loved ones most prominently and others a close second. Human beings need one another to survive. I believe that the attributes of good will, honesty, harmony, kindness, and love are critical components to positive human development and that they must be caught and taught. Unless these attributes are properly developed, the dark side of human nature will take over. I have always held this viewpoint and find, the older I get, that this perspective shapes more and more of my decision making.

Rudy   I was never very comfortable expressing my feelings. That is still true today. My values are evident in what I do more than what I say. I decided to teach because students are the future of society. My discipline was math because I was good at it myself. Mathematics is the doorway to understanding much of the universe and is a very practical skill in the marketplace. If a person can do things like math well, he or she will be more likely to have a strong self-concept, make good decisions, and be a positive contributor in all aspects of life.

Rachel   As a little girl, I learned in Sunday School that God created me and loves me and that I should live my life in such a way that others can see that love in what I say and do. Some of those qualities to which I aspire include patience, generosity, forgiveness, hospitality, and a keen sense of purpose to serve my heavenly father faithfully. I became a teacher because I thought my values would have maximum impact in the midst of children. In retirement, I continue to put myself in situations where I can enjoy and influence others who are walking life's road.

Murrae   A good dose of work ethic, discipline, trustworthiness, and dependability are important values. They bring strength to character when life throws curve balls. Too many children miss positive influences in their lives that would enable them to thrive and strive in a rough world. I entered education to pass along those values that my parents taught me and that proved to be helpful in my life. I made my expectations very plain to students. They knew where I stood. Some rebelled at my standards, but most expressed appreciation for what I tried to do. Even today, in retirement, I work as a volunteer with troubled youth.

Defining success is evident in what retirees reported were their hopes and dreams prior to retirement. Goals signal important motivations and provide benchmarks by which to judge progress toward highly held ideals.

Heidi   Learning more about people who live in other countries was high on my list of retirement objectives. I wanted to see how people outside of my usual circle live, eat, think, and act. This meant more than a pass-through vacation. Home stays were a requirement, and I searched for programs that would provide more than a day or two in port or town. I figure the more I learn about others, the more I learn about myself. The better part of life is self-discovery.

Michael   I wanted to have a second career. I had attended career night at a local technical college. The fall I retired I started taking classes in retail floral programs. My long-time interest in gardening probably prompted the course of study, but my belief that the mind will atrophy unless it continues to learn is surely my prime mover and shaker. I graduated with my retail floral degree. The classes were tons of fun to take.

Lucille   My life changed radically when I retired. I finally had time to deal with some personal issues that I never took the time to face when my life was so structured and so busy. My husband and I first separated and then divorced. We sold our house. I began attending weekly meetings of an Al-Anon group that has helped me understand and deal with alcoholism. I am looking forward to a new life, including new relationships and jobs, as well as service and learning opportunities. This process of becoming excites me.

Eugene   My goals in retirement are not that different from what I adhered to as a superintendent. I want to make real contributions to people and organizations. I want to be missed (in a positive sense) when I leave. I want to live in a respectable fashion from a financial standpoint. I wish to know my own strengths and capitalize on them. I wish to keep on learning, stay busy, and remain interested in the world around me. In short, I want to count, not as a number but as a significant human being.

Mitzi   A successful retirement in my mind is not having my life run by shoulds. The freedom to be spontaneous is a critical success factor for me. It is hard to protect free time enough to be able to respond to opportunities. New doors rarely open unless some of the old ones close.

Burton   My retirement goals changed when grandchildren came into the picture. I spent decades trying to teach and influence other people's children. Why should I be any less committed to my own flesh and blood? Our travel plans and organizational commitments take a back seat to time with our grandchildren. Sometimes we baby-sit, go on hikes, play games, or cook in the kitchen. Sometimes we watch them play in Little League sports. Sometimes we invite them to our church for special events involving children, such as Christmas caroling. We know our place. We are not the parents, but we can love them as older adults who think they are very special and who let them know it in hundreds of ways.

Renée   Not many, or I should say any, of my values changed after retirement: respect for others, honor and honesty in dealing with others, hard work, careful planning (to avoid waste and the unexpected), care for my family and friends, trying to get the most out of every day, enjoyment, and appreciation of the life around me (natural and human). My advice is to relax, embrace your new life and enjoy it to the fullest, keep a positive outlook and attitude, and don't whine or complain. You have better things to do with your time and energy. Retirement changes the context in which lifelong values are played out, not the values themselves.

Retirees are quick to share their activities that demonstrate a set of values. Family is a prominent topic of conversation. Friendship is highly prized, as is service to others. So are learning, caring, and faith development.

Ivan   No one had compiled a good family genealogy. I took on this special project as a way of loving my children, grandchildren, and future generations. This proved to be a much larger job than I anticipated. I used my four sets of great-grandparents as source couples (all came to the United States from Norway). The ancestry has been traced all the way back to the early 1600s and late 1500s for some of them. I have over 2,500 entries on my computer. Not everyone shares my enthusiasm, but I've learned there is a time and place in the lives of most people when family lineage data becomes important.

Hannah   What distinguishes us as a family? What did our forebears believe? How did they live out their beliefs? I was too busy to pursue these questions before I retired. Most other family members are still working so I decided to capture firsthand stories of those living and recollections of those no longer living. This family history speaks less to who married whom and when than to what family members valued (value) and did (do). Stories vary regarding some long-dead family members. That surprised me and made me wonder what impressions this generation is making on the next. Perhaps these autobiographical sketches will help clarify stories in the future.

Paige   The fellowship of good friends is what helps make my retirement to enjoyable. Staying at home, alone, can be deadly to mind, body, and spirit. I consciously get out of my house every day, even to the point of programming shopping, banking, and doctoring on different days. Efficiency is no longer my goal. Relationships with people are most critical for me in retirement, especially since my husband died. This has always been the case for me, but now I must work at it. Maintaining old relationships and kindling new ones takes a good deal of effort. The support, camaraderie, and fellowship make each day special—the priceless gift of companionship.

Boise   I am an active sportsman, teach confirmation at my church, and serve as president of the local Dollars for Scholars chapter. All three require considerable time but each fits my beliefs and interests. I consult part time for a regional group of businesses that are interested in workforce training. Again, the purpose of this work fits a lifetime interest—promoting economic growth and development and providing meaningful labor for people. I have volunteered for one-day activities when asked, but I have been careful to avoid overcommitment. I also try to keep golf leagues and cabin time sacred in the summer. The key for me is twofold: matching choice activities to valued purposes and keeping good time balance among them. Oh yes, it is wonderful to take an afternoon nap while reading the newspaper. Taking care of my health fits in there, too.

MY JOURNEY

In my childhood, I heard many expressions that spoke volumes about values. Here are some examples: "What you do will speak more loudly than anything you say." "One act of kindness is better than a thousand words." "Work for the night is coming." "Remember your Creator." "Be patient like Job." "Think before you speak." "Look at the ant, you sluggard." "Remember the

Golden Rule." "Your reward will be in heaven." Such phrases usually accompanied commentary about right and wrong actions; each gave moralistic or spiritual content that gave clear direction to act in one way and not another. Sometimes they felt like a straight jacket; at other times, they resolved a dilemma without much thinking.

CONCLUSION

Values are the bedrock upon which life decisions are made, consciously or unconsciously. When values are well identified in mind and examined closely in context, they guide the thinking process and make the resulting decisions more consistent, internally and externally.

Most life choices, however, are not between good and evil but between apparent goods: Will this or that action be better for you, me, the institution, state, society, country, Earth? These smaller distinctions are also helped by value clarification and commitment, though not so precisely. Values espoused but not followed are but talk without bite. Retirees readily name many values, including the following, and just as quickly, acknowledge a host of temptations that try to undermine them in direct and subtle ways:

- Caring
- Generosity
- Equality
- Social justice
- Individuality
- Community
- Integrity
- Honesty
- Learning
- Responsibility
- Initiative
- Restraint
- Faith

QUESTIONS TO PONDER OR DISCUSS:

1. How comfortable are you in expressing your life values? What has been your experience in making life values explicit?

2. What values (ideals) did you hold dear all during your life as professional educator? Which of them do you anticipate will continue into retirement?
3. How will retirement open new doors for you in living out your value commitments?
4. To what extent will you match your retirement goals and critical life values? To whom or with whom will you be accountable in this endeavor?
5. What life values are most difficult to realize in retirement? Why?

CHAPTER SEVENTEEN

Recognizing the Values of Individuality and Community

Individuality and community are like two smaller river systems that flow together to make a mighty waterway upon which a democratic society can depend. Educators recognize both the central place of individuals in our society and the critical role of community. They value them, teach about them, and model them in their own lives.

A major draw of the profession is the chance to enjoy and contribute to individuality and community, keeping the river flowing at high levels. Individuality champions the entrepreneurial spirit, creative juices, and work ethic. Community puts the premium on cooperation, joint effort, and communal needs and objectives. Both continue to be highly prized values in the life of retired educators.

Willard When I retired, I thought I was so ready to leave the hustle and bustle of the classroom. Little did I realize that six months later I would be substitute teaching, in large part because I missed being with students. Each one is different; each one is unique. Each one carries a spark, a potential, a challenge that requires my best creative thought.

Loretta So much of my life revolved around school that the prospect of retirement filled me with a feeling of emptiness. I knew that staying in my condo day after day would be like a prison sentence. Even weekends away from school seemed too long sometimes, and my mind continued to think school thoughts even during holidays. What would be my new connection(s) in retirement? Who would fill the void? I didn't want to cut off my school associations without having new relationships with people well in place.

Lopez I was already working part time on weekends in the tool department of the local Sears when I retired. At first, I spent my weekdays at home in my own woodshop. After some weeks, I took note that on Thursday and Friday my spirit was lighter. Even my wife noticed it. We determined that I needed a better mix between the isolation time in my shop and the people time at the store. I've increased my hours at Sears and spread them over more days of the week. My work for pay is not an interruption but a much-needed break that brings more people into my life.

Mabel   When I think back, I retired from school and immediately scheduled much more time with my grandchildren. I visited their homes and invited them to come to mine. I fixed up the porch, making it a playroom. I sought permission from a neighbor for the children to use their swing set. I re-searched what hours the health club would allow me to take my grandchildren swimming. I marked their scrimmages and games on my calendar. My immediate family filled much of the time and space that once was occupied by school responsibilities.

Fran   Shortly after we retired, my husband and I encouraged others in our age group at church to start a new group called Second-Halfers with these intended purposes: fellowship, spiritual growth, learning, recreation, travel, laughter, enjoyment, and service to others. Four years later, our mailing list is about 150 people strong, and the variety of activities (about seven or eight over the course of a year) brings in forty to eighty couples and singles each time. Different members take charge of each activity so the workload is relatively light. We find great joy in the things we do, places we go, but especially the companionship and camaraderie at this time of our life.

Perry and Mardell   Our retirement dream was to build a log home in the deep woods. Our dream became reality within two years. We lived in a small tent-trailer on the site and did most of the work ourselves. We sold our city house and thought we were in heaven. Now we are talking about a weekend cabin in the city. What we have in mind is a small condo or apartment so we can worship in our old church, see our friends without bothering them with overnight stays, and go to sport events, plays, weddings, and funerals, and shop at leisure. In the summer months, we have loads of visitors at our log home but the isolation in the winter is hard to take. We have discovered how important it is to us to be part of an active community. An occasional visit doesn't do the trick.

Among the reasons given by most educators for selecting education as a career is their commitment to community service. Schools open their doors to youth to help them prepare for multiple roles in adult life, and staff members are employed who accept this mighty challenge. Salary, alone, draws few into the profession or keeps retention high. Altruism is the primary moving force for educators from the first day of work to first day of retirement. Not surprising, therefore, are stories of many educators who during their retirement years continue to give community service, but in new venues.

Merle   Long ago I came to this conclusion: My happiness lies not in giving to organizations, hoping for promotions or status, nor do I work for another person because he or she pays me. Too often this orientation leads to self-pity or the feeling that I am an object for hire, rather than a valued human being. I think the primary purpose of work is personal development. My growth as a person expands when I work and serve others. Retirement, for me, took work out of the formula, but I still need to honor the service ethic because that is how I grow and achieve true happiness. I'm busier than ever in retirement—and very happy, too.

Russell   I am quick to volunteer as a poll watcher because elections are democracy in action. I'm glad to meet my neighbors and am proud when former students show up to vote. I am busier than you might guess. We have many elections in our state: national elections, state primary elections, and school board elections in the spring. Many referendum issues are taken to voters in special elections such as school operating levies, school bond issues, and park and recreation proposals.

Raymond and Geri   Our state counts on citizens to help keep the roadways looking nice. Trash accumulates alongside major highways. We put our name in for a section of roadway not too far from where we live. Three times a year we don orange vests provided by the state and pick up the garbage. The highway department posts signs with names of volunteers so people know the two of us value refuse-free highways and are doing our part to keep them that way.

Annabelle   I served on the zoning committee for our city for several years while I was yet working in the schools. When I retired, several past and current members of the committee urged me to run for the city council, noting that I had good experience and would have extra time for those duties. They helped run a successful campaign and continued to give me counsel and support in this new role. Unfortunately, politics has a bad ring to many people, but it's how the public business gets done in America. I'm proud to serve our community in this way and am often asked to speak in social studies classes.

Gladys   Our school district has a community service department that provides adult education courses and programs that serve identified community needs. When I retired, I was invited to serve on the community services advisory committee. The role is a good one for me because I am active in community life (a good listening post) and know most of the school employees who oversee the programs. Trust levels are high, and our reputation for top-quality, lifelong education is well known throughout our state.

Salina   Two generations ago, my grandparents made their living working in sugar beet fields as migrant laborers. My parents did not graduate from high school, but they pushed my siblings and me to do well in school. Three of us became teachers and one a nurse. Shortly after my retirement, our church decided to prepare meals, serve them, and to do clean up in a downtown community center where over 400 poverty-stricken people go for their evening dinner. I volunteered to be one of the workers, and soon thereafter, became the program coordinator for our church. I remembered what it is like to be hungry and homeless and believe we are our brother's keeper.

Wilber   Financial problems in our school district prompted cutbacks in school bus transportation. Students must now walk farther to bus stops, and the larger numbers so gathered can use some adult supervision. The request for volunteers struck a chord with me. I don't want children to be hurt by bullies or passing cars. Even though I am now retired, I still get up early every morning anyway, and this is a good opportunity for me to stay in touch with the younger generation. If I can't make it, I know of other retirees who can. We are a dependable lot. Of course, we have weekends, summers, and holiday periods off so our community service is only 180 days a year.

Scott and Valerie   Last summer we took our camper and settled into a beautiful national park as volunteer overseers. We didn't do heavy maintenance, but collected the fees, gave advice about trails, and kept our eyes open regarding fires and the like. We met hundreds of interesting people, heard their stories, and marveled how our national parks help people of all ages enjoy the out-of-doors and stay in touch with nature. Our own children and grandchildren came to see us in our temporary home setting. We were able to stay beyond Labor Day because we're retired. The leaves were absolutely gorgeous in the early fall.

MY JOURNEY

Community first made itself known to me as a farm boy, in a variety of ways: two farmers talking by the roadside for thirty minutes (one in a pickup truck and the other by an idling tractor), no place to park in front of the hometown café for coffee at 9:00 A.M., everyone in town turning out for a funeral, a tattle-tale call to my parents that I was burning rubber around the town square, a full church Sunday morning and night, bidding beyond reason at the auction of a friend, and when I came home on a weekend, inquiries from neighbors on how college was going. I belonged when I conformed. I was chastised when I resisted its authority over me or deviated too much from its norms. I desperately wanted its love when no other community recognized me, appreciated my individuality, or met my heart needs.

CONCLUSION

In retirement, value of individuality and value of community are given renewed life, like rain on parched soil and wilting crops. Individuality is expressed and enjoyed in the pursuit of individual interests, performance of part-time work, and contributions made through volunteer work in community. Community can be the by-product of these activities or be sought readily in its own right in religious settings, civic organizations, and even sporting events.

Unfortunately, many retirees face drought conditions at one time or another in retirement. Usually later in life, physical, mental, and emotional health problems arise for many retirees that severely cramp opportunities to express their individuality and enjoy community. Discovering, creating, and enjoying individuality and community is the true work of retirement and is sometimes the most difficult to sustain. Some recommendations from long-retired educators follow:

- Celebrate your long-used "personal" skills such as listening, speaking, and writing by using them as long as possible.
- Be willing to develop new skills or relearn old skills that will allow self-expression in spite of challenging conditions. Push back all the harder when ill winds blow.
- Initiate new activities of interest throughout life, as conditions permit, that will help define you as an individual.
- Maintain old friendships and associations. Seek out and foster new friendships and associations.
- Diversify social connections, thereby stimulating present moments in life and expanding the probability of rich associations later in life.
- Establish a spiritual connection with a higher power that yields companionship, comfort, and communication until the last breath of life.

QUESTIONS TO PONDER OR DISCUSS:

1. To what extent do you cite individuality and community as factors when someone asks you why you are in education?
2. What has made you a distinct, unique, special human being during your working years? Which of these elements will continue into retirement? Which will be expanded? How?
3. Who or what is giving you a sense of belonging to community within your work environment? Which one(s) will you miss the most following retirement? Why?
4. When you retire, where will you turn to express your individuality and to meet your need for community? Which connections are already in place? Which ones may need cultivation?
5. In what ways, if any, do you anticipate giving service to community when you retire? How important is service to others in your retirement years?

CHAPTER 18

Continuing the Value of Caring

An abundance of caring is a signal quality found in most educators. This propensity to step outside of oneself, to see, hear, and appreciate another human being, increases insight, aids communication, and promotes excellence in instruction. Learners served by caring educators feel more important, demonstrate higher motivation, learn faster and better, and reveal greater confidence about their future. That is education at its best.

Career educators are professional caregivers in a school setting, but this foundation of caring comes less from training than from an attitude formed early in life and developed more fully through life experiences. As such, retired educators often find themselves as caregivers in retirement because the practice of reaching out is so deeply engrained in the heart that there is no escape, nor a wish to do so.

Roberta   During my long career, I found the greatest satisfaction in working with low-achieving students. I see myself in each of them. Until my junior year in high school, I was a poor student, prompted by home troubles, frequent moves, and gang influence. A teacher helped me face up to new possibilities in my life. That new path eventually took me into education. I'm now retired, but I still work with troubled youth through a program called Step Up, which matches caring, successful business people with capable but underachieving students in their senior year. I can tell you story after story of kids who have been rescued by relationships with good role models. My debt to that caring teacher in my life will never be fully paid.

Faye   I left the classroom after five years to become an elementary principal. The pay was higher but the work year was longer. One of my goals was to help other teachers, particularly first- and second-year teachers, survive the early challenges of classroom management and become excellent teachers. I was nearly a dropout myself, saved by a principal who saw my potential and helped me bring order out of chaos. His caring and expert advice convinced me that a principal can play a powerful role in support of teachers on the front line, and that became my theme song until I retired.

Actually, it still is, because principals I know call me when they have a teacher in trouble, asking if I would be willing to spend some time with him or her. I haven't taken on the title of consultant, but that is truly what I am.

Yoshi   Wrestling was my high school and college sport. When a school district offered me my first teaching position, the contingency was to be the head wrestling coach also. I accepted the contract and soon learned that coaching creates a powerful bond with athletes. Our heart-to-heart talks included not only wrestling but also academics, disciplinary issues, and life choices. Before long, school counselors were sending me recalcitrant students. Wrestling was like a boot camp for them. I look back today on hundreds of students who have become good fathers, good workers, and good citizens because athletics helped turn them around. Though I am retired, I still volunteer as an assistant coach in the wrestling program, helping today's troubled kids.

Rita   My first teaching assignment was in grade six where, to my dismay, I learned that two of my students did not know how to read. They were totally frustrated and acted up negatively to gain attention. I did my best but felt ill prepared to help them. My deep concern for them and guilt over my own inadequacies helped me decide to do my master's degree work in reading, which turned into my life's work. As a reading consultant, I helped instructors teach reading more successfully and worked directly with students who needed my extra help. I remember one dyslexic student who not only graduated from high school but also finished high in his class at the Air Force Academy. I believe that good ends are determined by good beginnings. Now that I'm retired, I volunteer to read to young children in our local library and provide tutorial help for a few students whom my former colleagues refer to me.

The caregiving spirit that propels people into education and helps maintain high energy levels through a career is frequently put to work in community settings following retirement. Readiness to help others in need isn't limited to the school setting.

Toni   My work as a school social worker made me fully aware of families in trouble, even in our middle-to-upper-class suburban community. Very surprising to many residents, a few students lived in cars when they got in trouble at home. Caring for children and youth was more than a job for me. I felt it was a calling, a mission. I volunteered in a local food shelf program and now serve as part-time coordinator. I also donate some hours to an organization called Families Moving Forward.

Reidar   Some of my retirement time is spent driving meals to shut-ins. Meals on Wheels serves hundreds of older people in our area, and I find much satisfaction in this volunteer work. Each meal I deliver is accepted graciously, and I know our short conversation in the kitchen may be the only face-to-face talk many will have that day. As a high school student, I remember Christmas caroling in homes of elderly members of our church. One elderly man cut up an apple and gave each of us a slice. I wondered if it was the last one in the bowl.

Constance   My marriage ended midcareer. Most of the time my husband was a kind and thoughtful man, but he had a temper that could flair up almost any time. He would lose self-control and hit me. When he refused to get help, I got out. That was long ago, but I am very sensitive to the plight of battered women. It happens in the best of homes, not just in low socioeconomic areas. Not too far from my apartment where I live as a retiree there is a battered women's shelter. I volunteer there three evenings a week to assist with in-takes. My heart goes out to these women and their children who suffer abuse. This loving support and caregiving is what they need. My own spousal abuse and long-time work with children helps me develop rapport with them. They arrive so confused and frightened.

Floyd   My wife and I retired to Colorado to be close to our daughter, son-in-law, and two grandchildren. After settling in, time began to weigh heavily on my hands, so I looked for a volunteer job that would be a good fit and found just the thing. A regional park gives nature tours to visitors. As a retired science teacher, I know the woods, enjoy teaching, and relish being out-of-doors. I took some orientation classes and now spend two days a week leading groups on nature walks. I care about the environmental issues and believe each generation must be taught anew how to preserve our natural resources. This role as a tour guide allows me to live out my passions, be with people, and breathe fresh air. What could be better?

Perhaps the most common caregiving in retirement is to loved ones, typically a spouse whose health has deteriorated. Many educators report going through this valley of hurt, discouragement, and grief. The sensitivity and patience gained as professional caregivers in education may not translate directly into care giving to adults, but the basic elements are well in place.

Clara   One year before my husband's planned retirement, he was diagnosed with Parkinson's disease. For three years, prescribed drugs helped to control his muscular movement, and we could easily go places and do things. Thereafter, our lifestyle changed dramatically. He needed help eating, dressing and undressing, going to the bathroom, and walking from point to point. When he began falling and slipping to the floor, I found I could not lift him (he's a big man) and tried to hire a health aide. But such private help is expensive and hard to find. I decided to put him in a nursing home where I visit him several hours a day.

Dewayne   I thought I had learned patience as a special education teacher, but the word now has a capital "P" in my life. A few years after we retired, my wife's eyesight began to deteriorate, quite suddenly, as a matter-of-fact. Surgery or corrective lens could not restore her sight and my eyes began to serve both of us. She asks me to describe scene after scene as we drive, watch television, or shop. She needs assistance when walking in strange places. Chores she used to do alone now require the two of us. In many ways, we have become much closer. In other ways, the added strain becomes apparent when little irritations turn into big ones. She's reluctant to learn Braille. We spend much time listening to books on tape.

Sonia   I shouldn't complain. We've lived a long life that has been free of health problems for the most part. My husband's heart started to show its age two years ago. He lost energy, became lethargic, and sleeps more hours each day. A pacemaker now regulates his irregular heartbeat. I am in charge of his pills, his diet, and his transportation to the doctor. He is forgetful and careless, especially when his depression is severe. I can understand all this with my head, but my heart is heavy. Once I was an advisor to high school cheerleaders. Now I try to be positive and enthusiastic with him and myself. The game clock is running down and our team is falling behind.

Joel   Let me share this story I got off the Internet about Jacob, eighty-five, and Gertrude, seventy-nine. Both had lost their spouses, had newly fallen in love, and were excited about their decision to get married. They went for a stroll to discuss their wedding and on the way passed a drug store. Jacob suggests they go in. He asked the man behind the counter, "Are you the owner?" "Yes," answers the pharmacist. "Do you sell heart medication?" "Of course we do." "How about medication for circulation?" "All kinds." "Medicine for rheumatism?" "Definitely." "How about Viagra?" "Of course." "Medicine for memory?" "Yes, a wide variety." "What about vitamins and sleeping pills?" "Absolutely." "Perfect," says Jacob, "We'd like to register here for our wedding gifts." Like the two people in this story, my wife and I in our older ages put pride behind us and do whatever it takes to live life to the fullest.

MY JOURNEY

Several years ago, my wife and I made a pledge to learn the names of all the kids in the neighborhood, to engage them in conversation, and be cheerleaders in their lives. (We believe a whole village is necessary to raise children.) We began to pay attention to them in little ways that showed we truly cared, and they have reciprocated in kind. For example, yesterday, I walked out the front door of our home to retrieve the newspaper. In the semidarkness of the early dawn, I saw a totally unexpected 4'-x-6' sign that stretched between two trees. The side facing the house said, "Happy 67th Birthday, Mr. Draayer." Later I learned that the children, two of whom are now in high school, waited until 11:00 P.M. the night before to be sure I was in bed, and that they left the number sixty-seven off the sign on the roadside just in case I didn't want people to know my age. Such loving care and attention every retired person should receive.

CONCLUSION

Caring is the value that moves self to second place in relationships. It is like glue that unites, cements, and preserves friendships. It is like a miracle drug that helps to heal, strengthen resolve, and make obvious that you are not alone on this earthly journey. Caring can be as simple and quick as a warm greeting, but often it requires hard work that competes with other life tasks and is not always appreciated. Caring is what brings educators into the profession and is what motivates and sustains career educators through the years. And the caring value continues its prominent place into and through retirement. Education retirees, with rare exception, are generous to the core. In retirement, the caring value is shown in thousands of ways, as illustrated below:

- Remembering birthdays of family members. Staying in touch with friends.
- Helping neighbors move and welcoming newcomers.
- Expressing thanks to others for their good work, attentions, and kindnesses.
- Contributing to worthwhile causes. Giving time and energy in community service.
- Eating disliked food that a friend has prepared or strange food brought by foreigners to a potluck.
- Driving someone to the airport when taxi service is readily available.

- Visiting the sick, listening to broken hearts, and praying for courage in another's life.
- Showing exuberance about someone's good news and congratulating him or her.
- Going to a funeral, expressing condolences, and hugging loved ones lost in grief.
- Spoon-feeding a handicapped person, or not giving your own spoon feeder a difficult time.
- Thanking, with a smile, the nursing home aide who brings the pills or changes sheets.
- Keeping a picture diary for each grandchild with a personal journal entry. Putting pictures made and sent by grandchildren on the refrigerator.
- Cheering a game from cold bleachers or clapping for all the kids at a long recital.

QUESTIONS TO PONDER OR DISCUSS:

1. Who was influential in your early life helping to establish the value of caring?
2. In what ways has your caring as an educator been revealed during your working years?
3. In what ways, if any, do you anticipate that your caring for others in the school setting will be continued after retirement?
4. What community situations might draw out your caring for others and prompt follow-through after retirement?
5. What experiences have you already had in caring for others in a family context? How do you think you will respond if or when extensive caring for loved ones comes into the picture?

CHAPTER NINETEEN

Practicing Lifelong Learning

Educators know that learning and life are like the two sides of a coin— inseparable. During professional years, educators reveal deep commitment to learning. Educators remain in education when other jobs might pay more. They commit many evening and weekend hours to correct papers, supervise school events, or prepare lesson plans.

Professional educators also know that to be most effective, they must practice what they preach about learning. The license to teach comes from much learning, and the renewal of licensure requires continued study. Education is called a profession because its members know a body of knowledge, demonstrate essential skills, show the right attitudes, and apply all three with fidelity and commitment.

The door of retirement doesn't end such practice. Retirement extends, broadens, and deepens learning. In a true sense, retirement doesn't close down learning; it enlarges, refines, and perfects learning.

Logan   Often my students asked me why I became an English teacher. I always told them that I loved reading stories as a youngster and came to appreciate how good authors use words and language so effectively. That hasn't really changed for me, even in retirement. The turn of a phrase to make a point fills me with admiration for both the writer and what is being said.

Morgan   Early in my childhood curiosity was deep within my nature. How did things work? Why do people think and act the way they do? What do mountains look like? (We lived in Illinois.) My parents told me I was full of questions. School subjects opened doors to understanding and satisfied my desire to know. Eventually, I came to the point of wanting to be someone who could make learning a life's work. What better than teaching? Retirement hasn't changed my basic nature, my curiosity. However, I now have more time to read subjects of my own choosing. You'll see one or more books at my bedside, in the den, on top of the kitchen table, and in the bathroom, wherever I'm likely to park for a while.

Jeffrey   I always envied fellow students who could memorize easily, think quickly, and remember the smallest details. I was an average student who had to work hard to get good grades. Learning for me was always a means to an end. I learned because it got me what I wanted or needed to have. I saw others around me who struggled to learn. I could empathize with them. I'm sure my sensitivity to the plight of others helped me be patient with slow learners during my teaching years. This focused, deliberate, and extended effort to learn continues to serve me well in retirement. Something new faces me constantly, including new computer programs, questions about health, and investment opportunities. I may not be the first to know the answers, but you can count on me to do good homework.

Roxanne   School came easily for me. I noticed early that teachers called on me when they wanted the right answer. I remember reading a teacher's comments on a term paper to the effect that I saw the big picture and made strong connective links. My parents told me I was bright but not to let that go to my head. Rather, I should use my gifts to help other people, possibly to teach. Eventually, I did become a teacher and loved class discussions where I could see lights go on in young minds. Not surprising, I suppose, is the fact that in retirement I am a member of two book clubs and serve as coteacher in a class for adults at church. Lifelong learning is more than an expression of doing. For me, it is the essence of being.

Formal opportunities to learn during retirement years are abundantly available. An entire industry called Elderhostel has developed that focuses on retirees, caters to travel interests, and opens doors to learning twelve months a year. Not to be forgotten are colleges and universities who have no maximum age limits on students pursuing degree programs or taking individual courses of study. Also, local school districts typically provide adult education classes through community education programs. Human growth and development through formal learning remain alive and well for many retired educators.

Leah   My husband and I have participated in twelve Elderhostel programs. You can access the catalogs by mail or over the Internet. Really, they are a combination vacation and education. Eight of our twelve have been in the states and four have been in other countries. We meet so many interesting people. They come from other walks in life. We learn from experts about subjects that interest us. We've studied stars at night in the Arizona dessert, exotic fish and animals in the Galapagos Islands, and Shakespeare in England. Some courses provide a physically active program including extensive swimming, snorkeling, beach walks, hiking, biking, and mountain climbing. Elder-hostel experiences are helping to fill the current chapter of our lives.

Rollin   We don't have much extra money for distant travel. Besides, we don't want to be gone and miss the activities of our grandchildren. We opt for local community education classes. The catalog has everything from Wood-working 101 to the construction of websites. We've studied history's turning points and futuristic thinking. There are classes on how to write, how to buy and sell, and how to invest wisely. Travelogues bring exotic places to our front door. We meet new and old friends and neighbors around our common interests. This is the best retirement bargain in town.

Delores   When I retired, I began to receive study/travel brochures from my college alumni association. About four times a year, they sponsor study/travel trips to various parts of the world, places I have never been but have always wanted to go. The first time I registered, I invited a friend to go with me. I dis-covered that people who sign up for these opportunities are also interested in meeting new people, as well as seeing and learning new things. Now I go on one trip per year knowing everything will meet my expectations, the travel, study, and social connections. I would go more than once a year, but the price tag would eat too big a hole in my pocketbook.

Warren and Marilyn   During our working years, we attended national edu-cational conferences that took us to distant cities and provided seminars around our professional interests. After retirement, we joined a civic club that holds their annual convention in various countries of the world. We attend these annual meetings along with thousands of other people. We feel right at home with the general session pageantry, hearing stimulating speakers in breakout sessions, and having opportunities to mix with people socially all during the day and especially at the end of the day. Often we extend our visit for some va-cation time in the host country. Later, we report back to our home club so there is a kind of accountability for what we have seen, heard, and learned.

Informal learning goes on throughout life, including retirement. Without realizing it, new knowledge is acquired, understanding grows with more life experiences, and appreciation for human diversity expands. Many retirees ex-press a new sense of openness to the world around them and consciously take the time to become better observers and commentators on the changing scene.

Jocelyn   It wasn't until I retired that I fully realized how cloistered I was during my career years. My time was spent in one building with a very stable faculty.

My reading focused on my field of discipline and even holiday periods were largely spent in graduate classrooms or conventions for educators. Most of my friendships and social connections came from the school scene. I loved my preretirement life and wouldn't change a thing, but I consciously have broadened my exposure to the world in retirement. There are local lecture series advertised in the newspaper. Authors come to town to give readings or talk about their books. Plays, musicals, and dance productions flow through the calendar year. Gradually, my friendship circle has expanded and I find my calendar is chock-full of events and new people who enrich my life.

Arvid   One of my jobs as an assistant principal was to patrol hallways between classes, keeping my eyes peeled for trouble. Watching the interaction of people in crowd situations nearly became an obsession. Sophisticated crowds during intermissions at an orchestra concert and the hodgepodge of people moving about during the seventh inning stretch at a baseball game can be as entertaining as the musical performance on stage or baseball play on the field. Even ordinary trips to the grocery store can be extraordinary outings if watching people is consciously part of the fun. Another related interest of mine is a good read in a biography or autobiography. There is no end to learning about habits, styles, motivations, and perspectives of people.

Bart   I seldom objected when the administration assigned me to teach a different course. It was harder work, of course, but I learned so much in doing the preparation. Looking for something new to pursue and do has continued in my retirement life. In the midst of tradition and routine, a little serendipity goes a long ways to keep life interesting. For example, hobbies can be changed over time to include new subjects or activities. I spent some time building model airplanes and included visits to air shows in the region to see full-sized planes and meet the pilots. A few times, they took me flying. I joined an archeology club for a few years. I accompanied them in local digs and once signed up for a major expedition to New Mexico. Currently I'm into photography and the newest digital cameras. An open mind is never a dull one. For me, all of life is one adventure after another.

Bernice   My husband tried to get me to use the Internet prior to my retirement. I was just too consumed by my work responsibilities to spend the time or really become comfortable using it. Following retirement, my excuses were gone and I found getting up to speed wasn't nearly as complicated as I thought. My first sale over the Internet (on e-bay) was my mother's gold watch, which I hardly ever wore. I participate occasionally in chat rooms and seek all kinds of information from websites. Through e-mail, I am much more in touch with our foreign friends because I don't have to go to the post office for special stamps. Forget that old cliché that there is nothing new under the sun. For me, of late, it has been using the full range of Internet services.

Adie   There are so many worthwhile causes and campaigns that interest me. During my career, I worried what people might think if I associated with the wrong crowd or would spent my time and money on less-than-popular initiatives. No longer! I am retired now and say "to heck with what other people think!" I am living according to all my convictions, not just some of them. Prolife is one of my causes. Another is the environment. Still others are world hunger, discrimination, and peace initiatives. These are more liberal stands, I know, but what good am I if I keep my thoughts in a closet? When election time draws near, I support those candidates who reflect my views. My house is on a corner lot and election signs fill the space. Not a day passes that I am not busy learning, serving, and relishing what lies ahead.

MY JOURNEY

Learning for learning's sake has its place, I suppose, but my work ethic and task orientation seem to link most of my learning to doing and achieving practical ends. I learned about fertilizers and insecticides on the farm to improve and protect the crops. I went to college to prepare for work away from dirt, danger, and heavy lifting. I studied education to teach, change lives, and improve society. I entered administration with the mind-set of servant-leader, learning how to operate institutions more effectively and efficiently for people working in them and being served by them. Even writing this book exemplifies my learning value because I want to learn from others about the retirement road and become a better traveler in it.

CONCLUSION

The desire to learn is a key differential between good and poor students. Likewise, a strong commitment to learning is one of the criteria to qualify as a professional. For educators, learning is like the drum in a marching band—it creates points of reference, signals change, and establishes momentum.

Some learning, like casual clothing, is so ordinary and comfortable that it barely registers attention. Other learning, like athletic gear, is functional and helps the mind achieve some clear, specific objective. And yet other learning, like sophisticated party clothes, places the mind in a whole new framework dancing with ideas. All of which says learning is inseparable from life in all its various forms. Educators in retirement accept this truth, recognize its imperative, and continue to learn by multiple means, as has been done throughout life. Cited are some examples:

• Waking up and moving limbs for body feedback, checking the weather and selecting clothes, and looking at the calendar and deciding how best to get everything done.
• Reading the newspaper and deciding what to share with others as the day unfolds.
• Opening e-mail on the Internet, deciding what to read, delete, pass on, or reply to, and printing off appropriate materials for self or others.
• Assessing literature from charities requesting money and determining which ones to support and to what extent.
• Studying others in the family, on the street, or at places of business to gauge their thinking and feeling and make judgments how best to act or react to accomplish this or that purpose.
• Putting oneself into group situations involving personal interest, work, or community service and deciding what one knows and still needs to know in order to make a difference.
• Gathering information relating to housing, transportation, investments, spending, and relationships and making decisions carefully.
• Assessing at the end of day what did or did not go according to plan and determining what will receive special attention tomorrow or be put on the back burner.

QUESTIONS TO PONDER OR DISCUSS:

1. What kind of learner were you in elementary, middle, and high school?
2. Has your attitude toward learning changed over the years? If so, how?
3. Will learning in retirement for you be more or less important? Why? Upon what do you base your judgment?
4. What have been long-established interests in your life? Which ones, if any, are directly related to your educational career and which ones, if any, are quite independent?
5. What formal learning opportunities have you pursued during your working years that are outside of your career requirements? Which ones are you likely to continue, or initiate for the first time, after retirement?
6. What informal, more casual, learning experiences appeal you? To what extent have you already pursued them? Which ones, if any, will you pursue with vigor following your retirement?

CHAPTER TWENTY

Applying Faith in Dimensions of Retired Life

Age-old questions of purpose, meaning, life, death, and the hereafter come into closer view during retirement. Faith reactions and responses of retired educators fall across the total religious spectrum. For some, religious faith plays a central, commanding role in every aspect of life. For others, theology and religious faith are real to them but more abstract, like a distant mountain covered with haze. Still others reject religion outright, and purport to no particular religious doctrine. Finite faith categories are impossible to catalog, except that nearly all retirees admit to doubt now and then, especially in times of severe testing, such as illness and death. The faith journey, while varied in its expression, is clearly evident in lives of retirees.

Mildred In my retirement, I bought a condo in Florida one block from a Catholic church. The proximate location was the overriding factor in my decision. I go to daily Mass, see the steeple from my bedroom window, and feel a warm presence in my heart. I have been a devout Catholic all my life and would feel like a fish out of water if my church wasn't close by.

Alice I should take you into the den and show you the books on either side of my reading chair. If you did such checking over the years, you would see a gradual change in book titles and authors. I still like a good read in a novel or autobiography but religious books are found more frequently these days in those stacks of books. I don't think that I'm searching for answers as much as I need reassurances about my faith.

Ivan I can easily share my faith with you, for it touches every aspect of my retirement. One of my earliest memories is going to church each Sunday morning and evening with my parents. Imprinted in my mind was that, in the beginning, God created all things. This center-circle position of God is also my heart's conviction. I believe God continues to be fully engaged in the seen and unseen universe, including every aspect of human life. Retirement has given me more time to think about my faith but not much else has changed. I hope that my faith will remain strong and carry me through whatever tests lie ahead.

Ole   Sure, I go to church but not all the time. I also shop, see the doctor, go to a movie, fish on lakes, and play cards with friends. Everything has its place in my life, and each serves a purpose. I don't like associating too much with church folk who dress up nice on the outside, talk about piety, but say and do things to people during the week that reveals hypocrisy. I don't want my religion to be a lie. I go to church less to socialize than to be reminded that I am more than flesh and bone. I am spirit, too. Church helps me pay respect to my Creator and be more mindful that my walk is more important than my talk.

Patricia   My chosen profession of education probably grew out of the idea that service to others is evident in a well-lived life. During my working years, I did not—and now in retirement do not—turn to religion per se for direct guidance on how to use my time, spend my money, or treat my neighbor. My ethics, my goals, and my future are defined in large part by the culture in which I live and help to create. My parents were members of a local church but attended irregularly throughout the year. I mostly remember Christmas and Easter services. I know the rituals but have never made a deep, personal connection. My parents stressed the Golden Rule and defined the good life in humanitarian terms more than religious ones. I believe the rewards for living the good life are here and now. They may be extended in some fashion throughout eternity but all that is ambiguous to me.

Alicia   My spiritual journey has taken me to the Eastern religions in which God is one, infinite-impersonal, ultimate reality. I am persuaded that all life is cyclical and hierarchical. I am a reincarnation of something that was and will, in turn, return into another life form after my death. Ultimately becoming one with the One will be attained, discarding matter, and ultimately ending the reincarnation and achieving true peace and love. Meanwhile, my current self, my essence, is bound to Earth. I want to live and act in ways that will accomplish my ultimate destiny. Meditation is central in my life, but occupational pursuits have been necessary to clothe and feed myself. Retirement enables me to pursue spiritual paths more fully and attentively.

Beth   I view every day in retirement as a precious gift to be received with thanksgiving, entered with enthusiasm, used in fruitful service, and credited to God. I want to be a good steward, using my time, ability, and resources to His honor and glory. Through Christ, God's Son, I shall one day enter heaven, not because of my good works, but through grace that comes to me by faith in Him. My life purpose is to be His instrument in the world. Retirement hasn't changed my faith perspective one iota.

Ronald   I don't think I have lost my faith in the midst of my present troubles. More likely, my faith was never fully developed in the good times and this fact wasn't exposed until recently. Within a year and a half, I lost my wife and now live alone. I left my profession, received the news that my daughter has multiple sclerosis, and watched my stock portfolio decline over 35 percent. I identify with Job in the Old Testament of the Bible. Now I know firsthand that this life can be filled with suffering, loss, and hardships. My long-held concept of God who loves me, cares for me, and abides with me has been turned upside down. I feel adrift at sea. The sunshine has disappeared in my life. Storm clouds are everywhere. I yearn for a beacon light to help guide me through this rough water.

Dag   I believe a person must look internally for answers about life, rather than externally to long-established religions. The self in conjunction with community is the critical factor in determining one's destiny and that of society at large. A natural, upward evolution takes place when one's self-concept is strong and interactions with family, neighborhood, and community at large are positive. Humankind can thereby be lifted to ever-higher forms of existence. My beliefs in New Age possibilities led me to education as a career, and in retirement, continue to motivate me to learn more about myself and to relate in new, exciting ways with the community around me.

Amy   I have always believed that the essence of me is my spirit. I view my body as a temporary house for this spirit, and when I die my spirit will continue to exist not just in the memories of people but in an eternal existence with God and other spirits who in their lifetime acknowledged His power and grace in their lives. I do not agree with those who say human beings are physical matter only. During my life, I have tried to feed and nourish my spirit just like I take care of my body. As my physical self ages, my spirit remains forever young. Retirement is part of my outside world, unpredictable and changing all the time. However, my soul, my inner essence, has time and space limitations only while I am living. Whatever my state is or becomes during retirement, my future existence as spirit is secure.

Many educators point to specific postretirement decisions they have made that are clearly tied to their religious beliefs. Restrictions prompted by daily work schedules are removed. Religious values are lived out in new ways and sometimes in new places.

Ryan   Habitat for Humanity has been a perfect fit for me in retirement. I can find home-building projects almost anywhere in the United States so my desire for travel is satisfied. There are few scheduling problems. Because projects are underway throughout the calendar year, I like to work with my hands and enjoy the companionship of others who are committed to good housing for everyone. Last, and most importantly, I believe each human being is responsible for helping, serving, and lifting up other human beings. Making this world a better place is one of the reasons I went into education, and retirement opened the door to additional avenues of service.

Emily   In my retirement, I have moved to a California community where more people think and believe as I do. Because so few other people in the Midwest shared my religious beliefs, I often felt isolated and alone during my working years. I am now learning much more about meditation from those who are well experienced and, of course, I have much more time to practice what I have learned.

Markus   All our married life, my wife and I have supported Christian missionaries in other countries. When they came home on furlough, we listened to their stories. Often we said to each other that one day we should visit them on site. After retirement, our first overseas trip was to visit some missionary friends in Africa. We stayed for a month, helping out in the hospital and local school. Lord willing, we will do this again and again. Now our daily prayers for them include specific people, problems, and needs.

Andrea   I volunteer many hours each week in a program for troubled children. Most of my time is spent in the office answering the phone, helping with mailings, and working on special projects associated with upcoming retreats and activities. The doctrine of separation of church and state puts restrictions on teachers in public schools. Privately held organizations working with youth, however, don't have these limitations and can address all their needs, including the critical spiritual ones. When I hear stories of kids whose behavior has turned for the better, I feel I am living out my beliefs without one arm tied behind my back.

Many changes in religious faith during retirement are not major conversion experiences. Rather, most retirees report slight shifts in how time is spent, who is included within friendship circles, and what is said in private conversation. Changes are sometimes evident in worship attendance, stewardship commitments, daily devotions, and selection of reading materials. Some changes can be significant departures from earlier life patterns.

Philip   I joined a men's Bible study in a restaurant on Friday mornings shortly after I retired. Frankly, I needed the social interchange, and the practice of rotating leadership week by week forced me to do additional home-work when it was my turn to lead. Once I read four books about the Apostle Paul because the study material stirred my interest. I rarely miss these hour-long meetings. One little plus is that I can order bacon and eggs off the menu, whereas at home, my wife has me on a fiber-only breakfast.

Maureen   School board meetings met on Monday evenings and that is when Women's Bible Study fellowship met. Prior to my retirement, I heard such wonderful things from friends who were in the group. After retiring, I sent in my registration for the start of the next study group. This serious study involves homework, honesty in small group exchanges, and accountability for spiritual growth. My work life was pretty hectic for so many years. Sorry to say, I cut corners in my spiritual development. Now there is a much better balance in my life.

John   I can't say I pray more in retirement. I just pray better. As my life nears its end, my sense of God is much more personal. In my mind and heart, I feel I am addressing God as a friend and talking to Him about everything in my life (family, health, relationships, local issues, world problems) rather that re-peating ritualistic prayers to a distant listener. I end these prayer sessions with a peaceful spirit and a positive readiness for whatever happens during the day. Prayer in these latter years has shifted from obligation to God to communion with God.

Chloe   Since retirement, no longer do students come into my classroom where I can treat them with respect and teach them what they need to know. My mission hasn't changed in retirement, just the venue. I believe adults must model to children how to live life, not just instruct them by words. Actions al-ways speak louder anyway. As a retiree, I now actively look for opportunities to interact with children in the neighborhood, at church, and while shopping. I call them by name when I can, ask them how they are doing, and compli-ment them when I see good things happening. I write notes, call on occasion, and let them know another human being other than their parents think they are special.

Sandra   I think the last miles in the life marathon carry the biggest life chal-lenges, require the most patience, and put new responsibilities right in front of my face. My faith helps me through the death of friends, my own health anxieties, and my concerns for family members. It is more than quiet prayer. It often involves figuring out what is the right thing to say to people who are hurting or grieving, spending time with children who are yearning for attention, and following through on commitments to church and community with enthusiasm.

Cynthia   While working, I found my faith being applied to big things like helping a child see potential in his or her life, befriending a soul who was lonely due to the death of a spouse, or facing a financial crisis that would cut vital services to students. Now, I seem to be into little things like doing my exercises, taking pills, and eating right. Much more attention is now focused on me. I'm beginning to think that it is easer to apply my faith to the big, visible things in life than it is to be a good steward about those little things that now keep me preoccupied.

Logan   Forgiveness plays big in my retirement. Younger people in their busyness often forget me. Older people can't hear, see, or remember me. They are reluctant to drive at night or learn how to communicate with me using e-mail. And I, too, can become so self-absorbed and self-centered that I become as bad as or worse than everyone else. I find myself having to forgive others, and myself, over and over again. Otherwise, I feel like I've fallen into a hole with no ladder out.

Fred   Much of my life has been spent in religious training, study, contemplation, teaching, and preaching. I am also doing doctoral work in gerontology. My conclusion is that there are three broad roads in faith life. Retirees can be found on all of them. (1) One road with many lanes follows the pleasure principle, pursuing things that make us laugh, keep us preoccupied, and provide pleasure. In a very narrow sense, it is an "eat, drink, and be merry" philosophy. (2) The second road with many lanes is one of faith where life is marked by worship and service. Mysteries remain and doubts arise, but trust in God or forces beyond our comprehension carry us through the best and worst of times. (3) The third broad road is followed by skeptics, agnostics, and atheists. For some of these travelers, life is a matter of continuous study but no final faith answers. For others, life is a joke and not to be taken too seriously. For still others, life is a burden to be endured. In the extreme, this latter road and its many lanes can lead to nihilism in which no values are held sacred, nothing is deemed knowable, and futility rides supreme.

MY JOURNEY

At different times, I have walked down all three of the roads outlined by Fred, above. As a full-fledged member of the Western culture where materialism is so pervasive, I am sure the pleasure principle guides much of my decision making. I trust that the middle faith road is where most of my footsteps are found, although my impressions in the dust surely reveal times of hesitation, plodding, dancing, and running full-speed ahead. My true joy is present there. I find abundant purposes and peace there. And, my ultimate hope lies there. Finally, I admit to moments and even longer periods of severe questioning. Are my beliefs a product of what I've been taught or is what I hold with conviction in my heart found there by revelation, inspiration, and divine providence?

CONCLUSION

Religious faith is part of the life experience for most educators. For many in retirement, faith life is explicit, highly verbalized, and personally experienced. For many others, faith life consists of a general attitude or orientation regarding a higher power but without vivid detail or personal history. For a few others, faith life is seen as an anomaly generated by insecurity and perpetuated by institutions having limited merit. Broad categories such as these don't begin to describe the full scope of religious beliefs held by retirees. Regardless, the starting and ending points in one's faith make a tremendous difference in answering deep, probing questions about creation, purpose, life, death, good, evil, and other faith-based issues.

Often, retirees report a religious shift as the years of life mount, usually in the direction of more attention to religion, theology, and faith. In retirement, time is less structured, health is more problematic, and the certainty of death is proven by the literal burial of friend and foe. Contemplations of why, what for, and where to questions increase in the later years of life. Among the many faith pathways shared by educators in their retirement are these:

- Going deeper into one's religious beliefs, long held or recently acquired. Striving for a closer connection, a higher sense of commitment, and a more faithful adherence to spiritual powers and principles that comprise the religious domain.
- Retaining public observance of one's faith life, such as consistent church attendance, worship, and support, and struggling privately with old and new faith-based issues, such as celibacy, homosexuality, the death sentence, abortion, and stem-cell research.
- Exploring faith walks of other people and cultures. Incorporating their insights as well as one's self-revelations into a religious faith that is privately held, eclectic in nature, and consciously or unconsciously applied in daily living.

- Acknowledging intellectually the important place that religion plays in the lives of other people, but denying or disregarding such a role in one's own life either by conscious argument or benign neglect.
- Engaging oneself in open and honest dialogue with other people who share a faith heritage and are willing to admit doubts and explore difficult life questions within that tradition.
- Hiding, as much as possible, from one's conscious, thought-troubling faith questions, hoping to be spared firsthand experience with pain and suffering, and a belated search for answers.
- Concluding that no one faith, above all others, has a true pipeline to truth but respecting the journey of others and putting oneself more comfortably in one camp than another.
- Living simply day by day in trust that a higher power is in control of every aspect of life and death and that such purposes will one day become fully revealed.

QUESTIONS TO PONDER OR DISCUSS:

1. How would you describe your faith journey as a young person? Who was instrumental in helping or not helping you to form your religious foundations?
2. What current religious convictions do you hold most dear? How have they changed over the years?
3. Given your faith perspectives, what changes, if any, will this factor play in your retirement decisions?
4. What life issues, if any, are most pressing during retirement years that faith may (or will) be called upon to address?
5. Who will you seek out to help answer your deepest faith questions or with whom will you ponder matters of faith during retirement years?

POOLING RETIREMENT WISDOM
FROM EDUCATORS

My research put me in touch with hundreds of retired educators throughout America that I had met over forty-five years of work as a teacher, principal, superintendent, university lecturer, and educational consultant. Our conversations were singular, and sometimes repeated, in order to help the retiree recall his or her firsthand experiences and enable me to draw a portrait of that person's thinking, feeling, and perceptions of the journey. Previous chapters have included portions, and sometimes just snippets, of these conversations. Each helped portray how individual educators come to terms with retirement, first in anticipation, second through the formal act of retiring, and third with the ongoing transitions in retirement years.

As might be expected, the pronoun "I" was used throughout the text, except in the case of married couples, in which "we" more accurately portrayed the retirement story of two people living together. Clearly established is the fact that every retiree has his or her own retirement story, will bring personal validity to the experience, and will usually share it openly and honestly with the promise of anonymity.

In section V, the final one, it is now possible to overlay these individual recollections, reflections, and recommendations one on top of the other. Lost is the individual story; instead a group story emerges like a kaleidoscope of bright colors. Generalizations are extracted that add a greater measure of predictability for those who are approaching retirement, or who are already retired, and want a broader frame of reference in assessing retirement.

Chapter 21 bundles the individual conversations of retirees into collective reflections and generalizations about retirement. In chapter 22, the stages of retirement are recounted not as absolutes for every retiree but typical periods of sojourn for most retirees. Literally, a different approach is taken in chapter 23. I become introspective about my own retirement journey. I peer into my own head and pour out my heart. In many ways, this chapter is like a self-directed pep talk, a challenge every retiree must take on sooner or later. Chapter 24, the last chapter in the book, summarizes in succinct form the wisdom gleaned from straight talk with hundreds of retired educators and supplies some cheerleading for your own walk.

CHAPTER TWENTY-ONE

Capturing Collective Reflections and Group Generalizations

Earlier chapters included portions of communications and dialogues with over 300 retired educators across the country. Their experiences, perceptions, and voices about retirement are instructive. The cataloging and analysis of their straight talk about retirement yield the following reflections and generalizations about retirement.

EDUCATORS WHO LIVE LONG ENOUGH DO RETIRE, EVENTUALLY

Retirement for some educators comes early. Most others make the decision later when many coworkers are retiring. A few educators prolong the date of retirement as long as possible. Retirement comes first to mind as a choice, second to heart as a feeling, and third as a volitional act that forever changes one's life. Like the onset and end of puberty, there are no magical dates for retirement, just a broad span of time defined as eligible for retirement. All educators who live long enough eventually retire, usually on their own timetable.

MANY FACTORS CAN MOVE RETIREMENT INTO THE FOREFRONT OF ACTION

Educators often read about new or expanded opportunities in retirement or hear about them from colleagues. The possibilities within retirement come together like iron filings pulled by a magnet to a center point. Stories from colleagues who are already retired can whet the appetites of future retirees. Finally, retirement programs at the state or local level sometimes provide special retirement incentives that catch the minds and embolden the hearts of prospective retirees.

Less positive forces also can stimulate or force early retirement of educators. Funding shifts, revenue declines, changes in political power or administration, policy shifts, and supervisory conflicts prompt some retirements. Unexpected or long-festering health problems, weariness or exhaustion from advancing years, increased work expectations, and downward trends in performance reviews are also factors in some retirements. Turnover or retirement of work associates, salaries and wages that do not keep up with inflation, and retirement programs that actually freeze or reduce benefits with additional working years are also identified and blamed for retirements. Typically, educators name more than one factor in stating reasons behind the decision to retire.

RETIREMENT IS A MIND AND HEART DECISION

The concept of retirement is as common as an old shoe, but the full reality of retirement for many educators pinches like a new shoe—too narrow, stiff, and uncomfortable. Faint whispers of retirement heard only in the recesses of the brain return the subject to mind, again and again. The loud banging at the door by personal illness, family crisis, or mounting public critics can make retirement seem like a long-sought escape or a heaven-sent savior. Resistance to the retirement idea, if initially present, begins to lessen over time and is followed by cognitive reasoning and language that moves retirement from plausibility to possibility to probability to actuality.

Human beings react at some emotional level to all changes in their lives, and, especially so when a life-altering change is on the horizon. Retirement is like a second adolescence. Emotions rise with the prospect of fresh independence and the freedom to go, do, and be. They fall when attention is focused on what will soon be left behind or be significantly altered. Up or down, the emotional swings are dramatic, short-lived, and somewhat frightening.

Some emotions in retirement come from the core of human insecurity and fear, like fierce warriors in battle dress, rough, loud, and threatening to peace of mind. Other emotions associated with retirement are soft and lack clear definition, like dancing apparitions barely discernable to the eye. These vague feelings of happiness and peace attach themselves to fondest human hopes and dreams without a full support structure in place. Mood changes associated with retirement can make normal seem like a friend who departs suddenly without a set date for return but who, in due time, reappears with a great suntan, calming words, and a full basket of reassurances.

EXPLICIT QUESTIONS AND ANSWERS AND HELPFUL HANDHOLDING PROVIDE PEACE OF MIND

Retirement, like major surgery, is likely to be most successful when the skillfulness of procedure and the psychology of people are included in advance preparations, actual implementation, and long-term follow through. Educators about to retire raise many questions that can be answered very specifically and factually by checking with experts whose job it is to know what, when, and how. For example, state retirement officials are knowledgeable about pensions, including payout options, amounts, starting points, duration, and changes over time. District office administrators know about severance pay, health plan options, insurance coverage, pertinent state laws, and local contracts relating to retirement dates as well as the protocols associated with retirement. Financial planners provide updates on investment income and retirement strategies. Like good procedures in medicine, there is a well-traveled path of factual questions and corresponding answers for educators preparing for retirement.

RESOLUTION VARIES

Retiring, however, involves much more than nuts-and-bolts questions and answers; retirement, like human anatomy, is surrounded by human psychology. Retirement transitions are easier, faster, and more productive when the psychology of change is recognized and put into practice. Expressing doubts, fears, hopes, and excitement relative to retirement puts feelings out where they are more fully acknowledged by self and observed by others. Friends, associates, and family members can listen, give feedback, provide support, and express reassurances. Retirees already familiar with the retirement road with its many forks can describe how and why they made their decisions and how they have fared.

Retirement is much more than a legal and physical separation from an institution and career pursuit. It is a complete change in place, purpose, and people. As such, a host of questions come to mind, deserve answers, and are addressed by knowledgeable authorities. But much more than facts and logic are involved in retirement. There is also a vulnerable, human side in which the mind deals with doubt, the heart with anxiety, and the spirit with constantly changing red, yellow, and green signals.

RETIREMENT SETS A BANQUET TABLE THAT IS
FULL OF DELECTABLE CHOICES

Scanning retirement possibilities for most educators is like skipping into a brand new supermarket, credit card and senior-citizen discount in hand. Shelves of goods dazzle the eyes, and somewhat beguilingly, they entice shoppers to think big, spend freely, and forget the reckoning that is part of budget management.

Many educators report that retirement, in the early stages, creates a sense of the surreal in which previous checks and balances are readjusted in the direction of more time, new options, and greater choices. Like a campfire's afterglow, a benign period of bliss is experienced in which some self-pampering, personal indulgences, and long-delayed plans, often recreation or travel based, are activated.

Then, reality hits like a morning headache after a wonderful night on the town. School friends and associates are no longer close at hand to express daily greetings. Adrenalin rushes from challenging students, curriculum debates, and office deadlines no longer come from the workplace. Established routines for the retiree are broken without new ones yet in place, and the puzzlement is like that of a shopper who cannot find his or her car in the midst of a mall's parking lot and stands bewildered, uncertain what to do next.

The voids felt by retirees in early retirement are not always resolved quickly or easily. The complexity of choices can be frustrating. Everything is interrelated. One option looks good but will limit or eliminate other options; decision making is more complicated than first imagined. Furthermore, time that seems so expansive in the first blush of retirement is easily absorbed by daily necessities of eating, sleeping, and personal hygiene as well as ongoing commitments to family, neighborhood, church, and community. Many retirees state this lament: "Where did all the extra time go?"

Some retirees attempt to open these time boundaries by selling their house with its yard upkeep and household repairs and buying a condo or townhouse in which others are paid to do the maintenance. Still other retirees take the additional step of moving away, geographically, from long-time social contacts and commitments. Some retired educators take both steps at once. But all retirees eventually come to the realization that time in retirement is not really a variable any more than it was during preretirement years. They learn that the biggest change in retirement is not the time factor, but the number and type of choices that are available and the freedom to choose from among them.

Scanning of long-range retirement activities may occur before retirement or is delayed temporarily for some weeks or months following retirement, but nearly always, retirees engage fully in the exploration process within the first twelve months of retirement. Most commonly selected activities fall into four broad categories: hobbies and personal interests, work assignments inside education, work opportunities in the private sector, and volunteer public service. Like a young child in a candy store, most retirees make one or two choices and relish multiple samples within them.

Delight is the emotion expressed by nearly all retirees regarding their initial retirement choices. This seems to hold whether (1) they elect personal pleasures, continued work commitments, or voluntary activities in community life, or (2) they aim for a purposeful balance among the entrées. Over time, some retirees shift their attention and time commitment to different activities, but the one comment heard more than any other is this: "I have never been more busy or happy in my life." Whether this is selective recall or honest appraisal, retirees' descriptions of how they are spending time is invariably positive when their choices correlate with their values.

RETIREMENT'S FOUR GREAT CHALLENGES

As I just noted, retirees are willing and quick to share how they choose to spend their time. However, retirees are much more reluctant to share openly four generalized areas of concern: finances, residence, relationships, and health. Each challenge area surfaces at one time or another during retirement—and sometimes all four at once.

Finance

Finance is the concern named most often as retirement approaches. Once the amount of income during retirement has been clarified and is turned into regular, postretirement payments, finance falls off the radar screen until later in life when health-related expense brings it back again for high-profile attention.

Educators whose incomes were fairly predictable for thirty or more years usually find that retirement income is more of the same. Furthermore, educators who practiced expenditure controls during career years carry them over into retirement. If financial troubles come, they tend to fall into one or more of these realms: poor investments, overly ambitious travel or housing plans, loss of dual incomes due to divorce or death, serious illness, and/or addictions like alcohol, gambling, or drugs.

Residence(s)

At the outset of retirement, retirees give considerable attention to the dwelling place but not with a high level of concern. Housing choices at this stage are many and choices are motivated by factors that are essentially positive. Later, when health issues prompt or force housing changes, concern levels can rise to the point of high anxiety and, not surprisingly, consume a corresponding commitment of time and energy. In particular, downsizing living spaces and/or moving away from mainstream populations can make a retiree feel like a prominent actor who is moved to stage left and assigned a minor part.

Relationships

Another challenge pertains to relationships. Overall, retirees report general satisfaction with relationships. If transposed to a line chart, the line remains relatively flat throughout retirement with occasional short and upward spikes that are prompted and encouraged by fun and joyful interactions. These can be reunions, birthday parties, anniversaries, visits by children and grandchildren, and special community events.

At times, the same line chart can register slight downturns in relationships like dips in the stock market, or on occasion it will show a precipitous drop because a valued relationship has ended. In these latter instances, the line reflecting recovery may stall or return very slowly to long-established averages or historic highs. Relationships, like the equity stocks, are very sensitive to changing life conditions.

In particular, almost all retirees report stress and strain in relationships when news of their retirement first circulates and when the actual physical separation from friends and colleagues draws near. After retirement, establishing new or expanded sets of relationships outside of the school environment sometimes takes more time and requires more effort than anticipated. Also, married couples who retire sometimes report a testy period as they adjust to more time with each other. Thankfully, most retirees report resilience in meeting these initial relationship challenges.

Conversely, the gradual or unexpected loss of friends, siblings, or a spouse through illness, accident, or natural causes significantly influences relationships, reducing the number and quality of associations and foreclosing intimacy unless extraordinary efforts are made to replace them. Painful losses of life companions at any point in retirement can take emotions to their lowest ebb. In due time, the capacity for resilience shows itself and the human spirit rises again.

Health

Health is the final retirement challenge faced by retirees. Even though retirement often extends for three decades or longer without serious health problems, health is an abiding concern and somewhat foreboding presence during retirement. As reported by the National Institute on Aging (U.S. Department of Health and Human Services 2002), body parts wear out in the last decades of life. Little aggravations like colds and flu bugs that once were weathered like small bumps and dips on the ski slope can turn into moguls that test resiliency and threaten safety. Generalized loss of vitality reduces the body's resistance to invasive viruses, bacteria, and cancer. The threat of accident climbs with reductions in ability to see, hear, and react.

Many retirees are reluctant to admit changes in health, sometimes to their detriment and even demise. Retirees also express considerable caution about diagnoses relative to invasive surgery and life-threatening health conditions. In such cases, seeking a second or third opinion is commonplace and advisable; such consultations, however, can sometimes delay diagnosis and fill future days and nights with anxiety and loss of sleep.

Clearly, retired educators in America today are concluding that they must become their own advocates regarding health care. They cite health care systems that are highly specialized and compartmentalized and that are spread out geographically, that often regulate length of office visits, use of diagnostics equipment and procedures, and dispensing of prescription drugs.

They note that health records may be centralized, but their careful review by a physician in a short visit can no longer be taken for granted. Prescriptions from different doctors for different problems can conflict with one another and compound adverse side effects for the patient. Many retirees are obtaining information on the Internet to help formulate questions to be asked during office calls. These may help identify health problems or to crosscheck prescribed medications.

The assumption of good health in the first half of life is not held so strongly by retirees who are in their second half of life. During retirement, appreciation of good health definitely grows. The greeting "How are you?" is asked with genuine interest and with no little trepidation. The response "Great!" provides reassurance and is accompanied by relief. Most other answers will include a litany of health concerns. To retired educators, routine physical examinations seem more like major exams, and recommendations regarding good nutrition, exercise, and rest are taken more seriously.

Obviously, vulnerability to health issues can be exposed at any point in life, but the probability of health issues moving from abstractions to personal dilemmas increases exponentially with the passing of years. Given this likely change in lot, health-related issues are rarely out of mind for retirees. Commonly identified health topics are these: availability and proximity of health care, affordability of prescribed drugs, care and competence of health-care givers, new drugs and treatments, and health insurance coverage and cost. Like a ringing in the ear from tinnitus that cannot be stopped, finance, residence, relationships, and (especially) health problems challenge retirees in their own time and way.

VALUES HELD CLOSELY DURING CAREER YEARS REMAIN AND REAPPEAR IN RETIREMENT

Educators show remarkable consistency in their lives during working years, which continues during retirement. Retirement is not like a metamorphosis in which the butterfly turns into a cocoon or vice versa. Looks, gestures, manners, attitudes, biases, habits, tendencies, likes and dislikes, and basic personality type are essentially unchanged by retirement. Preferences for foods, choice of friends, types of interests, and political persuasions remain fundamentally the same. Affiliations with colleges, professional sports teams, religious organizations, and charitable organizations seldom switch with retirement. For the most part, subscriptions, reading habits, and favorite brands remain intact. Affections, disaffections, and opinions continue to be a constant, like bright stars in the clear night sky.

Educators continue to hold, espouse, and display most of the same values in retirement years that were manifested during their career years. This observation should not come as a surprise or shock, but what does change in retirement is the venue within which values manifest themselves.

Obviously, school responsibilities no longer command long hours of work, consume passions, or challenge commitments, but the deep-seated values that put educators into educational environments in the first place—and keep them there until retirement—are not to be denied. This is proven over and over again by reports from retirees whose choices in retirement about money, use of time, what to do, where to live, how to serve, and what to believe correlate so highly with their long-held values.

THE VALUES OF INDIVIDUALITY AND COMMUNITY

The value of individuality and value of community are held securely by professional educators. They honor the power and cite the benefits of individualism (self-initiative, creativity, and entrepreneurship). They also laud the power and influence of community (self-control, connectedness, and conviction). One is not raised unduly above the other during career years; rather, each is seen as a contributing force to American democracy and is spoken to in such a light.

In retirement, the place of individualism and place of community do not change in the minds, hearts, and actions of retirees. If anything, these values become even more pronounced. Retired educators, although no longer bound by school laws and board policies, continue, with rare exception, to respect the rights of individuals, accept human differences, and ascribe dignity and worth to all people. They frequently express their individuality by pursuing unique interests, finding secluded places to go, or building a place of retreat with their own hands. Simultaneously, the importance of community, that is, of belonging and contributing to people beyond self, continues as a deeply held value. Retired educators are found in almost every group of volunteers.

Supporting the common good is a closely held community value and is sometimes spoken like a mantra.

The Value of Caring

Caring is another deeply held value. Generosity, charity, and peacemaking are strongly held tenets of nearly all educators and continue to be lived out significantly by them in retirement. They gift their time, talent, and money to others. Rarely recorded are their good deeds that help individuals become better persons and help institutions, society, and the world become better places.

The caring value for educators is like the mounted flag in the schoolyard: predictable, trustworthy, visible, and so commonplace that a passerby rarely takes a second look. Yet moved to half-mast or absent by error, the flag will create a flurry of questions or protestations. The caring flag of retirees in education continues to wave tall, true, and red, white, and blue throughout their retirement. The patriotic tenor of retirement stories confirms this conclusion.

The Value of Learning

Learning is a very well-modeled value in the lives of professional educators. Learning opened the doors to college, licensure, and professional positions. Learning is further practiced during the career years with preparations to teach new courses of study and the reading of research about instructional methods. The vocabulary surrounding the learning value illustrates its importance—professional growth, advanced study, degree work, seminars, staff development, workshops, and continuing education renewal units.

As is expected, the practice of learning new things, exercised so continuously during working years, continues into retirement unabated. Examples include helping sons and daughters with their life's problems, managing investments, attending new personal needs, allocating donations among charitable requests, deciding what causes to support or fight, figuring out how to accomplish some home repair work, and weighing the consequences of spending holidays with one family and not another. For those retired educators who return to part-time work, learning is an inherent clause in all job descriptions.

In addition, retirement brings in a large parcel filled with new situations in which learning is essential, like deciding where and in what to live, selecting activities to fill unscheduled time, determining when to downsize and what to do with accumulated stuff, figuring out how best to initiate and foster new friendships in the face of a diminishing pool of daily associations, and coping with the changing health status of self and loved ones.

Learning during retirement years continues to be an important life value because it helps the retiree strive through the mundane, thrive through changing circumstances, and arrive at life's end with few regrets. I have come to understand through dialogues with retirees that happiness, satisfaction, and peace of mind come from a willingness to actively engage learning and deal effectively with those things that by design, fate, or default pose great challenges, and less so from the avoidance of things which can (and should) be set aside.

The Value of Faith

At some level, most educators recognize spiritual values in life. Here lay contributions of faith most commonly shared in the straight talk by retirees: promise, purpose, forgiveness, perspective, and prospective. Retirees readily cite how faith has been an especially meaningful or a powerful force in their lives. Examples are many, including conception and the miracle of birth, the magic of puberty, the marvel of marriage, the making of career decisions, the march (and clash) of ideas through time, the majesty of power wisely exercised, the management of retirement transitions, and the mystery of death.

The integration of disparate life elements helps human beings enjoy health, sense wholeness, and achieve peace of mind and happiness. Religious faith is how human beings, at least for the vast majority of educators, trace the connecting threads, discover meaning, restore strength for the journey, find comfort, and ultimately seek solace as life ends. However, faith is not always a steady force or an automatic given in lives of retirees. Many report periods of deep doubt, wavering, or even futility, especially in times of severe testing, such as after the loss of a spouse and during times of critical health concerns. Faith tenets are always in mind but not always felt in the heart.

For most educators, the search for faith values converges where it most often begins. Childhood teaching about faith becomes wholly accepted and more deeply internalized as one's own for all of life. For other educators, the search for faith values is more problematic; seeking can go outward to different religions or inward for self-development. And for still others, likely a much smaller percentage, religions are very suspect and not personal experiences. For them, their faith values remain a nebulous and disquieting possibility or are deemed to be an outdated notion, worthy of outright rejection. Regardless, most educators think more about religion and explore its depths more fully with the arrival of retirement, advancement of birthdays, and skirmishes in the midst of life challenges, particularly life-and-death health matters.

CHAPTER TWENTY-TWO

Identifying Stages in Retirement

No retiree's experience is exactly like anyone else's. The individuality of people, which is so obvious in infancy, adolescence, and teens and among career-centered adults, continues to be seen in retirement. Stereotypes are an injustice to the uniqueness of human beings of every age, including those in the fifth or sixth decade of life or beyond. However, individuals do exhibit patterns of behavior at all times of their lives that, in a collective sense, constitute stages through which nearly everyone passes. Such stages are evident in the retirement of educators, too. This chapter identifies and describes these retirement stages. A synopsis is found at the end.

Some caution here is advised. The stages of retirement described below are not arbitrary. Not every person will sense them or describe them in exactly the same words, nor does one stage begin and end in strictly linear fashion. Overlap and even repetition is commonplace. Some retirees even observe a cyclical rotation in which the stages repeat themselves but in new contexts or time periods. Regardless, there is uniform agreement among retirees that there are phases or stages in retirement even though there may be disagreement about the particulars.

STAGE 1: AWAKENING

Some educators can identify the precise moment when retirement moved from a generalized concept applicable to everyone to a very personal reality in their own mind. Often the word *it* describes retirement in the former state of mind while the possessive pronoun *my* is freshly used during the awakening stage. Whether sudden or gradual, the mind grasps the idea of retirement with a new consciousness that a major life change is about to take place.

The cortex of the brain sends the idea to the hypothalamus for an emotional rendering. How do I feel about this? Is there risk involved? Do I sense fear, pleasure, anxiety, relief, or combinations thereof? The reaction is never neutral. Sometimes the whole idea is pushed aside for a while as something too distant, big, or worrisome to be addressed immediately. Reactions send nerve messages outwardly that are translated into speech and body language and inwardly to muscles and body organs. Retirees often report restlessness, changes in digestion, and headaches, all signs of stress. Survival instincts are activated at some level; nearly always they include the asking of questions, which helps a person better understand options and courses of action.

STAGE 2: INVESTIGATION

Many questions are generated when the possibility—or, more likely, the probability—of retirement settles into mind and heart. Foremost among them are matters of finance. Can I afford to retire? What changes, if any, will be required in lifestyle? Will expenditures change during retirement and, if so, by how much? What can I count on from investment sources? Outside consultations help provide the answers and usually give reassurance. In fact, of those retirees in education who are one or more years into retirement, few mention finance as a major concern. Other questions typically pursued pertain to health coverage in retirement and how others who retired earlier spend their time. Much closer attention is paid to people who are already retired to learn from them.

But the most significant questions in the investigation stage are self-directed. If I am no longer a teacher, specialist, principal, or superintendent, who am I? Self-esteem and self-worth issues are raised to the highest levels by the prospect of retirement. Twenty or more years of early life are spent preparing for work and thirty or more years are spent doing it. Retirement is not just another life change. It is a gigantic hurdle for most educators because all the thought, training, and tenaciousness applied to career appear to be ending without a clear picture of what will replace it.

Leaving the workplace where one has spent many years is like pulling up an anchor rope without the ship's engine running and rudder activated. A person feels adrift. An important finding in the investigatory stage is this: Who I am is much bigger than what I am currently doing. Most people perceive this truth lightly before retirement but come to the point of believing it more fully during the investigatory stage.

Resolution to disturbances in the area of psyche also determines in large measure questions and answers about the next chapters in life. Do I retire now or wait longer? Do I consider either part-time or full-time work after retirement? What activities shall I pursue after retirement? (This is a particularly important question.) How will my choices be perceived by others and by me? Consciously or unconsciously, every question and answer is generated, answered, and tested in both the intellectual and emotional centers of being until a level of satisfaction emerges that constitutes the next retirement stage called peace of mind.

STAGE 3: PEACE OF MIND

Peace of mind is a relative term. On one extreme, the prospective retiree experiences a blissful state of thinking and feeling in which a carefree existence is enjoyed immediately or contemplated for the future. On the other extreme, he or she becomes so driven by future plans that little interest is shown in current position responsibilities. Persons on both ends of this continuum, and all points in between, accept the inevitability of the change.

They move more willingly into their retirement future because they have achieved sufficient peace of mind to look forward rather than back. Retirees report a slippery slope in this regard, two steps forward and one back and sometimes one forward and two back; nonetheless, the intent and overall direction is set, which is consummated in the retirement letter. The legal steps are then taken by school officials, opening the door to the next retirement stage, called celebration.

STAGE 4: CELEBRATION

Celebration can be private and public. Most retirees find some relief in doing drudgery work for the last time and note the passing with quiet acknowledgement, a little smile, or even a cheer. Self-consciousness rises about work routines, current events, and people who surround the retiree. There is a sharper emotional edge to almost everything that happens.

Friends, family members, and colleagues nearly always add their own creative ideas and energy to the atmosphere of change and new expectations. People stop by the classroom or office just to talk. Their conversation focuses less on current work and more on times past and plans for the future. Typically, parties or receptions are planned, sometimes small and quiet events that involve just a few people or sometimes extravagant affairs involving people who have driven or flown in from great distances. Money is usually collected to cover expenses and purchase a farewell gift. In addition, school districts often give retirees special honor in a formal ceremony in which employees of long service are recognized.

What is hidden in the midst of the obvious is a deep-seated sadness that what was will be no more. A transition in power, influence, and relationships is underway that cannot be stopped. The laughter, fun, and stories belie the

solemnity of planned events. The celebration stage provides ritual and ceremony for those who are not yet retiring to get used to the idea of separation
and to move on without the presence of a colleague.

Simultaneously, the celebration stage for the retiree is another important
step in learning to cope with the idea of retirement and its many ramifica-
tions and in bolstering courage for the road ahead. Emotions run high. Both
tears of sadness and joy release tensions. The retiree feels adrenalin filling
the bloodstream keeping energy levels high, sometimes late into the night.
The next morning, the routines of closing up shop return. Exhaustion is
commonplace because social interactions take additional time and regular
duties continue to press until the day after retirement when the next stage,
euphoria, takes over.

STAGE 5: EUPHORIA

It is over! I am retired. Those days and weeks leading up to the last day of
work were like a pressure cooker on full heat. Now I can do what I want.
Most retirees sense great relief and move into the stage named euphoria,
which can be short or long but which is seldom permanent. Things that bring
personal pleasure or satisfaction are undertaken, like extra-long baths, reading books without interruption, cleaning out the garage, fixing broken equipment, or making a hide-away place more comfortable. Very, very common for
retirees in this stage are extended vacations that are often paid, in part, by
monetary gifts at retirement functions or by severance payments.

The euphoric stage is temporary, but it fills an important function—
namely, making a clean break from the past and settling once and for all that
the past is the past. The next stage, introspection, overlaps with the euphoria
stage and soon commands center attention.

STAGE 6: INTROSPECTION

Introspection has its first budding in the months prior to retirement but the
flower comes into full bloom some days, weeks, and occasionally months following the last day of work. Options that are available on every front are
given close inspection, including finance, place of residence, relationships,
and activities that might consume newly available time. This outward survey
of possibilities can be quite casual and relaxed, be quite deliberate, or sometimes be desperate, if motivated by financial concerns or loss of self-worth
without work in the picture.

At the same time, the retiree looks inward to pinpoint interests, abilities, knowledge, skills, and possible contacts with whom to network. Deep-seated values are dusted off because external choices made will either confirm and manifest those values or give rise to dissonance, tolerated perhaps during income-producing years but seldom in retirement.

Sorting through alternative plans and the associated emotions can be a fun, joyful experience or be a laborious effort, but the process itself cannot be avoided. The promised peace of mind in retirement cannot be attained until the questions about what comes next are first identified, then narrowed down, and finally explored, which is the next stage of retirement.

STAGE 7: EXPLORATION

An educator's earlier history serves as the impetus for much retirement exploration. A long-ago vacation to a warm or cool place may trigger interest in a second residence in that location or even a permanent home. Alternative housing possibilities may also come to mind from people who some time back had you come for a dinner or visit. A volunteer experience of short duration, perhaps years before, can prompt curiosity about current opportunities to serve. Nostalgia about past work experiences can surface what was satisfying and rewarding, kindling exploration of part-time work in those areas. Occasional golf outings can turn into a golf club membership. If some past experiences are pleasing, and they coincide with opportunities in retirement, those particular choices are likely to rise in favor and be pursued more rigorously.

Also, exploration of options can be prompted by almost anything current, such as a friend's suggestion, an invitation from an old classmate, reading a newspaper article about a new product, seeing a work advertisement at a bus stop or grocery store bulletin board, or noticing a flyer seeking volunteers at a zoo, arboretum, or orchestra concerts. Whether requested or not, retirees find themselves on mailing lists to buy, to go, to serve, and to be. Likewise, e-mail messages can be unrelenting. Resistance and disgust win most of the time, but every now and then a chord is struck that prompts some action.

Exploration at some point moves from thought to motion. A telephone call is made, a drive-by is taken, or a commitment is made to self and others to try something for a while. In most cases, the mind is saying that if this doesn't work out, the world will not end. The pleasure principle is a very prominent criterion in the exploration of options and their evaluation. Retention of flexibility is another important consideration. Over time, these temporary decisions become more permanent, and the retiree is ready to move into the next stage, settling.

STAGE 8: SETTLING

Settling means acceptance and new stability. Satisfactory solutions arising from the exploration stage become more permanent. A new residence feels like home. Daily routines become predictable. Activities are repeated over and over until they move from unusual to normal. A retiree is likely to say, "In my new life, I . . ." The settling stage may come soon after retirement begins or be delayed for years following the last day of work. Every retiree's experience is different, but nearly all come to the point where they feel they have made a complete transition into retirement.

This settling stage may turn out to be of short or long duration. If good health persists, resources permit, and family situations remain relatively the same, retirees can remain in this stage for decades and perhaps for the rest of their lives. However, significant life changes usually interject themselves into the stability of the settling stage and prompt the onset of the next retirement stage, pulling back.

STAGE 9: PULLING BACK

The bottom line from the National Institute on Aging Information Center (www.nia.nih.gov/health/agepages/lifeext.htm) is this, "Currently no treatments, drugs, or pills are known to slow aging or extend life in humans." Retirees eventually feel the effects of aging, such as some energy loss, slower reaction times, and changes in sight and hearing. Walking up stairs can become more difficult, which often prompts a change in residence. Sometimes the pulling back is gradual, in which others are paid to do chores once done by the retiree. Some retirees reduce multiple residences to one; move to a residence that is closer to their children; find living quarters that are closer to shopping, banking, and medical facilities; or seek facilities specifically suited for elderly persons.

Change in place of residence reveals the abundance of things that have accumulated through the years, and many older retirees report a conscious effort to donate, give away, or otherwise dispose of clothes, equipment, and household items. Favorite mementos are carefully sorted, prominently displayed, and discussed with more frequency. Quite common is the giving of heirlooms to loved ones. Typically, investments tend to become more conservative and, quite literally, others are given more authority to handle one's financial affairs though such instruments as a power of attorney. Selling personal cars when driving of self and others is no long safe is another very difficult pulling-back act for most retirees.

The pulling-back stage can also be prompted by circumstances not directly related to the retiree himself or herself. An elderly relative may need personal attention and assistance that forecloses or requires frequency of travel by the retiree. Grandchildren or great-grandchildren bring new joy and pull at heart-strings; many retirees become involved in daycare or baby-sitting responsibilities and are less available to spend time with friends or pursue other retiree activities.

Most retirees point their finger at the medical conditions of themselves or spouses as the primary factor in pulling back. Obviously, the degree of pulling back is determined by the severity of the medical condition. In some cases, full-time nursing care is required, in which case the pulling back can be to a single room with or without a roommate. The pulling-back stage is nearly always difficult, even when physical pain is not present, because life treasures (including people, possessions, and pride of doing, going, coming, and self-care) are limited by age or handicap factors. Death is the final pull back and, for those who believe in life after death, the beginning of a new existence. This concludes the nine stages of retirement for educators in this study, a summary of which is found below:

- Awareness—Getting used to the idea of retirement intellectually and emotionally.
- Investigation—Identifying questions and getting answers about retirement.
- Peace of Mind—Deciding to do it, looking forward more than back.
- Celebration—Staring change in the face with laughter and tears.
- Euphoria—Usually short-term relief and pampering of self by fun things and travel.
- Introspection—What activities to pursue? What are my interests, abilities, skills?
- Exploration—Trying out different ideas.
- Settling—Finding a new lifestyle, accepting it, and enjoying renewed stability.
- Pulling back—Reducing responsibilities, unloading stuff, moving to age-appropriate living quarters, dealing with health-care issues.

CHAPTER TWENTY-THREE

Talking Turkey to Myself about Retirement

It is time now for me to turn inward and apply the wisdom gained from others to my own life. I must become a self-directed mentor who knows me better than anyone else and says, "Listen, fellow, what good is all this straight talk with retirees unless you begin to see yourself with new eyes and make some course corrections? If you value learning so much, why are you not seeing the insights of others as messages for yourself?" Not surprisingly, this chapter has been difficult for me to write. Putting introspection and honesty together requires courage.

In my own case, concepts have always been relatively easy to discuss, dissect, and distribute to others, but applying what I know in my own life is another story. I become so wrapped up, and perhaps warped, by yesterday that I am unable to see who I am today and could be tomorrow. I often recognize dissonance between what I say I believe and what I am willing to apply in my own life. This struggle for authenticity has been a personal battle throughout my life. It continues in the throes of retirement. Do others face the same paradox and challenge?

There I go again, working around the edges of the subject rather than going to its heart, lecturing aloud to an audience of unseen faces, rather than looking in a mirror. The mentor within me says: "Sit down for awhile. Talk. Tell me about the real you. What do the retirement revelations by others have to say about your own retirement? In what ways are you changing? What are your growing edges?" I know in my heart of hearts that, when these questions are answered, the ultimate objective of this book will be achieved in my life, and yours.

WORK IS SO MUCH A PART OF MY LIFE, OF ME, THAT I RESIST LETTING IT GO

Retirement, for me, is much more than just another change in life; it is a major upheaval in my thinking, feeling, and doing. My long-set beliefs and personal patterns of behavior are being shaken, much like the tremors of an earthquake. My landscape is changing, as are my points of reference. The dust clouds are beginning to settle. I can see that in retirement my life will be significantly different. Do I have the wisdom and courage to walk on this new terrain so altered by retirement?

I watched my parents work hard on our truck farm and I learned this work ethic, too. At the age of seven, I weeded one row of onions, hour after hour, with my mother on one side and grandmother on the other, each of them weeding three rows at a time. I heard my father railing about migratory workers in the farm fields who, he said, didn't work fast enough, work thoroughly enough, and work long enough.

Every day after supper, I heard my mother read a Bible story to her four children. One of the stories told of the fall of man, as related in Genesis, chapter 3: "The ground will sprout thorns and weeds, you'll get your food the hard way, planting and tilling and harvesting, sweating in the fields from dawn to dusk." She often said, "No rest for the wicked." As the oldest son, I became Dad's hired man until I left for college. Work on the farm was modeled. Work was required. Work was rewarded. Work was honorable. I learned that work was to come first; then, if time remained, some play.

My elementary teachers in the rural country school also kept work in the forefront of my developing brain. They used work-related stories in lessons, increased motivation by saying my parents would be proud if I worked hard, and smiled when my work improved. They wrote positive feedback on written work well done and rewarded me with high grades. I discerned early in life that the words *good work* and *good student* were parallel. I also learned good work pleases others, and me.

When I came home between college semesters with some relaxation in mind, I recall what my mother said: "College breaks are to do different kinds of work, not to do nothing." I did not protest too much. Unbeknown to her, the shift of work in my mind from a means to an end was largely completed already by the end of eighth grade. No wonder I resist retirement! It will end a lifetime orientation of preparing for work, going to and doing the work, and coming home from work. There is nothing I know better, or enjoy more, than work. What is left of me if I retire?

I NEED TO SEE WORK FROM A NEW PERSPECTIVE

Work is not the whole of me, but a part of me. Dare I believe this? My life is like a mobile hanging from the ceiling. Work, like a big weight, hangs from its center point. Other aspects of my life such as family, relatives, friendships, church, recreation, patriotism, learning, and community service hang there, too, but more toward the edges.

If I snip off the work leg, will my life mobile suddenly become unbalanced and lightweight, and, if so, in whose eyes? My parents, who are long dead? My teachers, who, too, have passed away? My former employers, who quickly hired capable replacements? If not them, who?

My wife says she wants to spend more time with me. My children invite me to their homes more often than I can accept. My grandchildren express delight when I hug them, read a story, or cheer them on in a game. My neighbors come around to talk when I'm out in the yard. My community reaches out with opportunities to serve. My church stresses moderation in all things. My God says, "Thou shalt have no other gods before me." Could it be that the tag *lightweight* would only be in my eyes?

SHARP DISSONANCE

My mind continues to hear messages about the importance of work. Are these old and long-playing tapes drowning out new messengers and messages? People who know me best, love me, and want to spend their lives with me are saying that work is part of my whole being, and maybe not the most important part at that. They remind me that my value is not what I do but who I am. They say, "Let me introduce you to a good man. He is a husband, a father, a grandfather, a brother, a friend, a believer, a cabin owner, a nature lover, a sportsman, a fisherman, a photographer, an organizer, and a reader. Oh yes, I almost forget, he used to work in schools."

This last notation really hurts. There is no mention of how long I worked (forty-five years) or what titles I held. There is no mention of honors bestowed on the school districts and me, the money I earned, the programs I initiated, or the thousands of students who graduated and are now full-time workers.

As I think about it, in the seven years since I left my position as school superintendent to work as a school consultant, the post has turned over twice, 80 percent of the staff has been replaced due to retirements, almost no parents at football games recognize me any longer, and younger neighborhood kids call me Mr. Draayer instead of Dr. Draayer.

One whole wall in the back room of our basement holds awards, plaques, and certificates from the year 1990 when I was named National Superintendent of the Year and gave speeches across the country. One picture shows me with President Bush in the Oval Office that he sent to me along with his congratulatory letter and signature. How many people do you think have asked to see these mementos in the last dozen years? The answer is "zero." More to the point, how often do I look at them? The answer is "rarely." Does this not help prove the fact that humans rarely acknowledge the past, must always live in the present, and should get ready for the future?

It is time for me to grip a new reality. I have been giving work more credence, more credit, more value, more priority in my life than does anyone who really cares about me as a human being. Isn't it time to back off from work, to get acquainted with the rest of me, and respond to new callings and challenges in my life?

RETIREMENT DOESN'T NEED TO TURN MY VALUE SYSTEM UPSIDE DOWN

I doubt my life values will disappear during retirement. I think my values are a constant. What changes is the venue in which my values play out. Interpersonal relationships have always been the context in which I try to practice many of my life values like virtue, honesty, kindness, gentleness, temperance, charity, peacemaking, humbleness, mercy, and forgiveness. This is not to say I always put a royal shine on them; indeed not. I confess to impatience, impertinence, impropriety, and a host of other negative temptations that often waylay a somewhat self-centered, type A personality.

In retirement, I know that more of my people interactions will occur in nonschool environments as I shift my time and attention to personal interests and activities in my home, church, and community organizations. My values will still be played out interactively, but with different sets of people. With whom I interact will no longer be a litmus test; politics are largely behind me. But how I interact with people I do meet will, forever, be a test of my character and core values.

I think retirement is helping me see the softer side of my nature. Already I am beginning to discern something I hadn't expected as I move more fully into retirement. In instances where I retain or have added a church or community leadership role, the organizational outcomes continue to be just as positive and I am enjoying the people and myself more.

RETIREMENT IS CHANGING THE CONTROL CENTERS IN MY LIFE

I know well the rewards of work: promotion, recognition, reputation, status, income, belonging, and purpose, but I am beginning to see more clearly the darker side. Work also directs, demands, delays, and, in some ways, destroys my wholeness. A full work schedule tells me where to be, what to wear, with whom to speak, how to speak, and what to speak. It also restricts my freedom to come and go. Conversely, my schedule in retirement is dictated by me unless I consciously and deliberately welcome others as life companions.

The added flexibility found in retirement is wonderful, but I have one new irritation: no readily accessible pocket calendar to record upcoming events. I wear no suit coat in which to carry it and I have not yet made the transition to an electric, handheld scheduler. My wife and I often find ourselves standing in the kitchen, each with a desk calendar in hand to coordinate respective dates and activities and to remind each other of commitments. With no efficient secretary staying on top of things, we are having conflicting date situations to work out. If anything, decision making in retirement appears to be more complicated because work can no longer be used as an excuse to say no and the variety of things for which yes would be the right answer seems to be endless.

These questions are helping me: How busy do I want to be? What do I really want to do? With whom do I want to spend time? I face them every day, several times. Sometimes I think it was easier when work controlled more of my life, but the thought doesn't last long. No, I don't want to go back to full-time work. I am beginning to become comfortable with the new me and what life calls my retirement.

HOW LONG WILL THIS GOOD TIME LAST?

An inner voice sometimes speaks subtly to me: "If you enjoy something too much, it must be wicked. If wicked, it will be punished in this life or the hereafter." My head discounts this as a very silly question (it isn't a question, more of a statement; how about the word, conclusion), but there is a part of me, emotionally, that knows life does not go on forever and that bad things do happen to good people, however they are explained.

Recently, I was sobered by the severe downturn in the stock market shortly after the Y2K scare of 2000. My investment portfolio took a hard hit: too much reliance on technology stock and too little diversification. Recently, my excitement about a pregnancy, a fourth grandchild, turned to sorrow when the fetus died for unexplained reasons. Then there is always the question about health for my wife and me.

My father lived to age eighty-seven as did his father, sound of mind to the end. However, Dad's two brothers and one of his four sisters died of Alzheimer's disease. My mother died of leukemia when she was sixty-four; arthritis in her joints had bothered her for years. What will be my fate, my health journey, my life's end? I am thinking about these things even as I enjoy the good times in retirement at age sixty-seven.

A month ago, I experienced pain in the joints of my left hand and my grip since then will no longer open a pickle jar. Is this arthritis, a genetic link? My internist says my blood pressure is perfect for a man of my age. My skin doctor says no more sun. My audiologist agrees that my hearing is getting worse, and my optometrist says my five-year-old glasses don't need changing. My financial planner says my portfolio is now steady, but for how long? Is this how it goes in retirement? Good news, bad news, ups and downs? Hundreds of retired educators like a giant chorus reply, "Yes. That is how things are in retirement."

WHAT DO I WANT MY RETIREMENT TO BE?

To my wife's utter amazement, I am not planning to draw up a written mission statement of goals and objectives for my retirement years. A few retirees do, and I could do it easily, given my historic orientation to the work environment. However, I am newly persuaded by the experiences of hundreds of retired educations, as found in earlier chapters, that the best course for me in retirement is to reduce the amount of structured time in my life and to be ready for more serendipity.

I want to become less concerned about products, tasks, or outcomes and to become more excited by human interactions in which family members, friends, and community members enjoy, uplift, and love one another. No longer do I need to prove anything. I can articulate an institutional or organizational vision. I can teach. I can lead groups of people. I can earn money. I can achieve job targets. Will I miss doing these things? Very likely or at least a little bit. Will I be able to grow into a new role, a new perspective, a new vision for my life? I surely hope so.

My leadership roles over the years put me among people and in front of people, but never did the role quite allow me to be one with the people. I want to laugh, cry, hug, and cheer with less reservation and caution. I hope for more intimacy with my wife, more fellowship with friends, and more open conversations with people I already know and others I will yet come to know. I want to live more fully in the spirit of love than to talk about the spirit of love. I want to be a blessing to others, as much as to be blessed.

EASIER SAID THAN DONE!

My old nature is in conflict with what I'd like my retirement to be. A few years ago, I had a terrible attack of kidney stones right before a speech to educators and community residents in Beach, Oregon. I threw up. I perspired profusely. My suit was wrinkled, my shirt stained, and my tie soiled. I remember standing before a spring-loaded podium and saying to the audience, "I'm very sick. Is there a hospital close by? I'm only going to give you the Rotary twenty-minute speech. Will someone then drive me to the hospital?"

You could hear a pin drop. They were all waiting for me to die before their eyes. I almost did. Twice I nearly fainted and leaned on the podium. It collapsed from my sagging body and popped up again when a shot of adrenalin helped me stand more upright. They took me to the hospital, the stones passed, and there have been no reoccurrences. Ironically, the evaluations of my short speech were the best I ever received. The only negative comment said, "He didn't take time for questions."

Was I heroic or foolish that evening? I was certainly true to my work ethic but isn't there a time when work should take the back seat or not even be on the list of passengers? This is my struggle, my clear choice in retirement. I want to let go of additional income-producing work and say yes to hope, trust, and security in this new time in my life, as captured by poet Robert Browning in the opening stanza of "Rabbi Ben Ezra":

> Grow old along with me!
> The best is yet to be,
> The last of life, for which the first was made:
> Our times are in His hand
> Who saith, "A whole I planned,
> Youth shows but half; trust God; see all,
> Nor be afraid."

CHAPTER TWENTY-FOUR

Summarizing Points of Wisdom

I have learned from these conversations, this straight talk. I hope you have as well. However, this Russian proverb speaks truth: "Pilgrim, there is no path. The path is made by walking." Each one of us cuts our own pathway into retirement. Based upon stories of earlier pilgrims, you and I can expect to feel apprehension, anticipation, excitement, fulfillment, occasional disappointment, and some sorrow on this journey.

The most critical variable in retirement is *attitude*. Educators who express the most happiness in retirement see today and tomorrow like a gift package to be unwrapped and enjoyed. They don't deny or forget the past, but they do make the present and future their primary focus. They acknowledge stages both before and after retirement and accept the fact that life is change and that retirement is progression.

When the right time comes for retirement, you will know it not by the passing of years but by what feels right in your own heart. The distilled wisdom coming from hundreds of educators who are already well into their own retirement can be summarized in these few simple, but profound, guidelines:

- Trust your instincts.
- Don't rush the day nor rue it.
- Talk it over with others.
- Express your feelings.
- Identify your questions and seek thorough answers.
- Acknowledge that you have earned and are worthy of a wonderful retirement.
- Depart with graciousness.
- Lay hold of new possibilities that best match your values.
- Include people, places, and activities among your retirement choices.
- Reflect moderation in all things.
- Strengthen faith, find courage, and set your own course.

During a typical transition into retirement, you are recognized and honored for long years of service, applauded for dedication to duty, and exhorted to think positively about the future. You are extended warm wishes for the journey by people who love you and have long known you as parent, friend, teacher, support person, administrator, and colleague.

You are in the limelight saying "Good-bye" to what was, and "Hello" to what is still to come. Also expressed are these heartfelt words: "Thank you!" "Good luck!" "It is hard to leave." "It is time to go." These statements are said to you, by you to others, and by you to yourself. Pep talks flow in every direction. Believe them. They bespeak great affection, appreciation, and hope. When tears come, some glisten with great memories and others sparkle with serendipity that comes with the new terrain and the freedom to learn, explore, go, do, and be.

You and I create our own retirement story, and we live it. If you journal about your retirement experiences, you will record thoughts and emotions much like those recounted in this book. Our similarities as human beings are much greater than our differences. There is great comfort in this fact because hundreds of thousands of educators have successfully made the transition from career educator to retired educator. So will you!

Educators learn from one another. You and I learn from those who precede us, as do those who follow you and me. Remember, your retirement and the decisions you make are like new billboards to the next generation of travelers, catching the eye, holding attention, and making an important statement.

This book is not finished because your retirement story is being written at this very moment. Your straight talk is waiting to be published in future editions, or perhaps in your own book. Already I can see the broad outlines of your story: you will rise to the choices, challenges, and commitments in your retirement, you will show courage in your retirement, you will reflect wisdom and share it with others who seek encouragement for their retirement journey, and you will continue to be part of creation's story; one generation to the next coming into its own.

Structured Interview Response Form

STRUCTURED INTERVIEW RESPONSE FORM

I am doing research that will help produce a book by this title: Retirement Straight Talk: Stories and Wisdom from Educators. *My aim is to touch both the head and heart issues.* To this end, the following questions will be asked person-to-person, if this is possible, by phone, or by written correspondence, if not. My idea is to enliven the text with real life stories, likely by boxed inserts and use of italics, *but with the source kept anonymous.* Your help will be sincerely appreciated. Please return the form to: Dr. Don Draayer, 5906 Holiday Way, Minnetonka, MN 55345 by mail, FAX (952-937-2387) or E-mail: dondraayer@AOL.com.

Name:_____ Address: _____
City: _____ ZIP: _____ Tel: _____
Retirement year: _____ Age at retirement: ____ Last position held? _____

1.0 Please describe **EMOTIONS** you felt at these times (elaborate freely):
- Months prior to actual retirement date:
- Time of retirement itself:
- Months/years following retirement:
2.0 What **QUESTIONS (CONCERNS)** did you have prior to retirement?
3.0 What "concerns prior to retirement" proved to be **REALITY** following retirement?
4.0 What **HOPES (DREAMS)** did you have prior to retirement?
5.0 What hopes (dreams) proved to be **REALITY** following retirement?
6.0 What **STEPS** did you take or **PROCESSES** did you follow as you approached retirement that you now recall as being very helpful?
7.0 What aspects of retirement did you not fully anticipate (**SURPRISES, GOOD AND BAD**)?
8.0 What deliberate **CHOICE(S)** have you made in these areas (and why)?
- Use of personal time:
- Continued work opportunities:

- Service opportunities:
- Place(s) to live:

9.0   What in your mind is a **"SUCCESSFUL" RETIREMENT**?
- Your definition prior to retirement:
- Your definition following years of retirement:

10.0 What **VALUES** did you hold dear during your career years that are still evident in retirement choices, challenges, and commitments?

11.0 What **ADVICE** would you most want to give future retirees?

12.0 Please add further thoughts and insights about retirement that come to mind and are not addressed heretofore.

Bibliography

Albom, M. *Tuesdays with Morrie* (Rockland, Mass.: Wheeler Publications, 1998).

Autry, J. A. *The Spirit of Retirement: Creating a Life of Meaning and Personal Growth* (Roseville, Calif.: Prima, 2002).

Bridges, W. *Managing Transitions: Making the Most of Change* (Reading, Mass.: Addison-Wesley, 1991).

Burgett, G. *How to Create Your Own Super Second Life: What Are You Going to Do with Your Extra Thirty Years?* (Santa Maria, Calif.: Communication Unlimited, 1999).

Canfield, J., M. Hanson, P. Meyer, B. Chesser, and A. Seeger. *Chicken Soup for the Golden Soul* (Beach, Fla.: Health Connections, 1999).

Cantor, D. W. *What Do You Want to Do When You Grow Up: Starting the Next Chapter of Your Life* (Boston: Little, Brown, 2000).

Carter, J. *The Virtues of Aging* (New York: Ballantine, 1998).

Cleary, D., and V. Cleary. *Retire Smart* (New York: Allworth Press, 1993).

DeBeauvoir, S. *The Coming of Age* (New York: Norton, 1996).

Everyday Psychologist. *The Psychology of Retirement: How to Cope Successfully with a Major Life Transition* (Arlington Heights, Ill.: Brodarts, 1999).

Freedman, M. *Prime Time: How Baby Boomers Will Revolutionize Retirement and Transform America* (New York: Public Affairs, 1999).

Gambone, J. *ReFirement: A Boomer's Guide to Life after Fifty* (Minneapolis: Kirk House, 2000).

Hampshire, D. *Retiring Abroad* (London: Survival Books, 2002).

Howells, J. *Retirement on a Shoestring* (Guilford, Conn.: Globe Pequot Press, 2002).

———. *Where to Retire* (Guilford, Conn.: Globe Pequot Press, 2000).

Koenig, H. G. *Purpose and Power in Retirement: New Opportunities for Meaning and Significance* (Radnor, Penn.: Templeton Foundation Press, 2002).

O'Shaughnessy, L. *Retirement Bible* (Indianapolis: Hungry Minds, 2001).

Otterbourg, R. K., and K. A. Kiplinger. *Retire and Thrive,* 2nd ed. (Washington, D.C.: Kiplinger Books, 1999).

Rich, P., D. M. Sampson, and D. S. Fetherling. *The Healing Journey through Retirement* (New York: John Wiley, 2000).

Savageau, D., ed. *Retirement Places Rated*, 5th ed. (New York: Macmillan, 1999).

Savishinsky, J. S. *Breaking the Watch: The Meanings of Retirement in America* (Ithaca, N.Y.: Cornell University Press, 2000).

Simmons, H. C., and E. C. MacBean. *Thriving after Fifty-five: Your Guide to Fully Living the Rest of Your Life* (Richmond, Va.: PrimePress, 2000).

Sinetar, M. *Don't Call Me Old: I'm Just Waking Up* (New York: Paulist Press, 2002).

Smith, M. H., and S. Smith. *The Retirement Sourcebook* (Los Angeles: Lowell House, 1999).

——. *101 Secrets for a Great Retirement: Practical, Inspirational, and Fun Ideas for the Best Years of Your Life* (Los Angeles: Lowell House, 2000).

Tate, V. D. *The Complete Teacher's Guide to Retirement Wealth* (Baden: Rainbows End, 1999).

Thomas, D. "Do Not Go Gentle into That Night," *The Poems of Dylan Thomas, Academy of American Poets* at www.poets.org (accessed 25 January 2003).

U.S. Department of Health and Human Services, National Institute on Aging. (January 2002) at www.nia.nih.gov (accessed 25 January 2003).

U.S. Department of Labor, Bureau of Labor Statistics. "Employment Status of the Population" (November 27, 2002): table A-1.

Whitney, C., and E. M. Bronfman. *The Third Act: Reinventing Yourself after Retirement* (New York: Putnam, 2002).

Whittier, J. G. *Songs of Three Generations* (Boston: Houghton, Mifflin, 1882).

Yogev, S. *For Better or Worse . . . but Not for Lunch: Making Marriage Work in Retirement* (Chicago: Contemporary Books, 2002).

About the Author

The long career of Dr. **Donald Draayer** in public education includes teaching at the elementary, middle, and high school levels. He also served as principal at all three levels and served as school superintendent for a twenty-four-year period. He taught graduate classes at the University of Illinois and University of Minnesota. Most recently, he has been an educational consultant in his own company, Experience PLUS, Inc. He has spoken to hundreds of audiences on behalf of the Search Institute of Minneapolis regarding developmental assets of children. His work and speaking have taken him throughout the United States, Japan, and China.

In 1990, Dr. Draayer was named National Superintendent of the Year and in 1998 was given the Distinguished Service Award by the American Association of School Administrators. The North Central Association presented him with the John Vaughan Excellence in Education Award in 1993; and in his home community, he was named Person of the Year, Senior Fellow at the University of Minnesota, and Minnesota Superintendent of the Year.

Dr. Draayer's wife, Mary Anne, is a retired educator. They have two grown children, three grandchildren, twins are on the way, and live in Minnetonka, Minnesota, a western suburb of Minneapolis, where they continue to be active in school, community, and church life. The inspiration for this book came from the hundreds of educators across America who enriched his professional and personal life and have shared their retirement journeys with him.

Endorsements

"Fresh insight, candid realism, and great reassurances about retirement are provided by Dr. Draayer, as he draws upon the stories and wisdom of hundreds of educators throughout the United States. He shares reflections on his retirement journey and invites the reader to learn from others who have previously walked this road. In this book, choices, challenges, and commitments related to retirement are laid out in an easy-to-read format. Each chapter ends with questions that promote self or group introspection. Every person facing retirement will find companionship, intimacy, and wisdom within this book's covers for one of life's major transitions."—Dr. Gene Carter, executive director and CEO, Association for Supervision and Curriculum Development (ASCD)

"In *Retirement Straight Talk: Stories and Wisdom from Educators,* Dr. Draayer has written an encouraging, supportive invitation, addressed specifically to educators, to think carefully about this important phase of life. *Retirement Straight Talk* offers its readers helpful resources and suggestions to prepare for the enormous changes brought on by retirement, along with the companionship and comfort of other educator's experiences. I believe the questions it raises will be useful for many educators, whether they are thinking about retirement, approaching retirement, or already retired."—Dr. Robert Bruininks, president, University of Minnesota

"Don Draayer is recognized as a distinguished student of American education. His thoughtful, thorough, and sometimes provocative study of the agony and ecstasy of retirement deserves your attention."—Dr. Carol Johnson, professor emeritus, Columbia University, Teachers College